KUYO CHICO

KUYO CHICO

applied anthropology in an
indian community

Oscar Núñez del Prado

with the collaboration of

William Foote Whyte

Translated by
Lucy Whyte Russo and Richard Russo

The University of Chicago Press Chicago and London

OSCAR NÚÑEZ DEL PRADO, a native of Peru, teaches in the University of Cuzco's department of anthropology where he has also served as chairman. He has published a number of articles in Spanish, and *Kuyo Chico* is his first full-length work in English.

WILLIAM FOOTE WHYTE is a professor in the New York State School of Industrial and Labor Relations at Cornell University. He is the author of numerous books including *Money and Motivation, Men at Work, Organizational Behavior,* and the classic study *Street Corner Society.*

The University of Chicago Press, Chicago 60637
The University of Chicago Press, Ltd., London
© 1973 by The University of Chicago
All rights reserved. Published 1973
Printed in the United States of America
International Standard Book Number: 0–226–60886–7
Library of Congress Catalog Card Number: 72–96621

To the memory of Allan R. Holmberg,
pioneer in applied anthropology in Peru and
unforgettable friend

Contents

Illustrations

MAP

PHOTOGRAPHS

Acknowledgments

I could not present this work without expressing my great gratitude to Dr. William F. Whyte, who, more than anyone else, is responsible for my decision to write this monograph. Perhaps it was the idea that social scientists with more training than I were working intensively in similar field situations that had made it seem premature to make my own experiences known, especially in terrain as rugged and difficult as applied anthropology. Perhaps I had not wanted to risk interference from the nit-pickers who are addicted to looking for and emphasizing only those aspects of a project which, in their judgment, are negative; who put forward opinions concerning things of which they have faulty or incomplete knowledge. I wanted to protect my work from the armchair critics, who almost always seek to justify their own inaction and to discredit the work of others. Furthermore, so many interests revolve around maintaining the status quo with respect to the *peasants* in Peru that the publication of my work would occasion the opening of a new battlefield for the politicians, theoreticians, and journalists.[1]

Professor Whyte not only persuaded me to write this monograph, but also arranged for me to have the necessary facilities and dedicated much time and effort to helping me in the organization and revision of the text. Above all, he was

1. For the cultural background of such worries, see Carlos Delgado, "Arribismo in Peru," *Human Organization,* vol. 28, no. 2 (Summer 1969).

a constant source of invaluable suggestions throughout the course of the work.

I also must thank my good friend Dr. José Matos Mar, who helped, with much enthusiasm and dedication, in the organization and revision of the text, and arranged for me to be provided with the necessary facilities through the Instituto de Estudios Peruanos, of which he is the Director. Drs. Whyte, Matos, and I got together around a tape recorder in Urubamba during several days in May of 1968 to develop the first version of this book. To this, Dr. Whyte added the chapter presenting the survey results, and he and I collaborated on the chapter concerning "Lessons for Applied Anthropology." A revised manuscript was then prepared and discussed at the Mexico City meeting of the Society for Applied Anthropology in March of 1969. A new draft was published in mimeographed form by the Instituto de Estudios Peruanos in February of 1970, and this served as a basis for discussion in a symposium in the Thirty-ninth Congress of Americanists held in Lima in August of that year. For the English edition, Dr. Whyte has written a new introductory chapter.

The support which I received from the Wenner-Gren Foundation, through the efforts of Dr. Whyte, has a special significance for me, since it was the same institution which supported the founding of the Department of Anthropology at the University of Cuzco in 1942, the department in which I later studied and received my professional training.

I want to make special mention of Juan Víctor Núñez del Prado B., whose field data and views were used extensively in the section on the spiritual world of the Indian contained in this work.

Oscar Núñez del Prado

Introduction
The Context of Kuyo Chico

William F. Whyte

This is a report, written primarily by the change agent himself, of an applied anthropology project in the highlands of Peru. Oscar Núñez del Prado, professor of anthropology at the University of Cuzco, and his associates intervened to bring about culture change and economic progress in the small indigenous community of Kuyo Chico. The intervention resulted in significant changes in the social structure of the community and in the distribution of power in a wider area surrounding the community.

The study is set in a context of Mestizo-Indian relations. In Peru those words refer to categories of people defined by culture and social class rather than by race. The author provides us with a guide to the categories of people involved in the project area, as these categories are defined by the people themselves.

The anthropologist begins by giving us a description and an analysis of the culture and social structure of Kuyo Chico at the time intervention took place. He presents a systematic description of the specific mechanisms whereby Mestizos in the district capital (Pisaq) maintained control over the Indians in the surrounding communities and exploited those communities.

The author then gives us a step-by-step account of the way he and his associates went about introducing changes in political and economic organization, in education, and in health. He analyzes the processes and results of the applied anthropology project to derive general conclusions that may be useful to others who plan to intervene to stimulate culture change and economic progress.

Along with a description and analysis of the intervention process, the report provides survey data designed to measure changes in the psychological orientation of the people of Kuyo Chico and also in their economic resources. Ideally, the first survey would have been carried out before intervention began, but, by examining the differences between Kuyo Chico and surrounding Indian communities, we can infer that the differences observed in the survey are to some extent due to the intervention. By means of a second survey, we can also examine changes that have taken place between the years 1964 and 1969.

Kuyo Chico in the Literature of Applied Anthropology

While the story of Kuyo Chico is full of human interest, we can better appreciate its value if we place it in the context of the literature of applied anthropology. We can distinguish three types of studies in applied anthropology, according to the role played by the anthropologist.

The anthropologist as critic. A large part of the literature is devoted to case studies of organizational or community change in which the applied anthropologist was not directly· involved at all. He describes the efforts to introduce change and seeks to show how the administrators of the organization or the political leaders of the community would have been better off if they had had access to the research data and advice of the anthropologist.

The anthropologist as consultant. As consultant to a government or business administrator, the anthropologist is in a position to show what his efforts in applying his research knowledge contributed to the organizational change process. In this role, the anthropologist has necessarily accepted the objectives of the policy makers and has sought to devise the tactics that would make their interventions more effective.

Introduction

The anthropologist as principal change agent. Here the anthropologist has been the chief strategist as well as tactician of change. He has determined some of the major change objectives and has directed the process of movement toward those objectives; at the same time, he and his associates have sought to document and analyze the processes of change.

Cases of the third type are rare in the literature. In a discussion at the Thirty-ninth International Congress of Americanists in Lima in 1970, Henry F. Dobyns referred to Kuyo Chico as one of the five most important projects of this type so far carried out.

Since two of the five cases cited by Dobyns were carried out in Peru, and since the Vicos project is far better known in the United States than Kuyo Chico, it may be of interest to compare the two. My purpose, of course, is not to determine which is the "better" project but rather to place Kuyo Chico in a context along with its better-known companion.

Vicos and Kuyo Chico resemble each other in that both of them were carried out in the highlands of Peru with Indian populations speaking different dialects of Quechua. Vicos is located near the city of Huaraz in the department of Ancash northeast of Lima, Kuyo Chico in the department of Cuzco near the city of Cuzco to the southeast of Lima.[1]

Vicos was an international collaborative project of Cornell University and the Indian Institute of the Ministry of Labor and Indian Affairs of the Peruvian government. Allan R. Holmberg, late professor of anthropology at Cornell, launched the Vicos project through an agreement with the Institute, then under the direction of the late Dr. Carlos Monge. Holmberg, William Mangin, William Blanchard, and Mario Vázquez served successively as field directors in Vicos. Vázquez, the Peruvian anthropologist, collaborated with Holmberg in the original planning of the project and came to be the key man with the project in Peru. Nearly all of the financing came

1. For the most comprehensive treatment of Vicos, see H. Dobyns, P. Doughty, and H. Lasswell, eds., *Peasants, Power, and Applied Social Science: Vicos as a Model* (Beverly Hills: Sage Publications, 1971).

from grants to Cornell by the Carnegie Corporation of New York.

Kuyo Chico was entirely a Peruvian project in design, execution, and financing, except for a brief period of Peace Corps involvement. On the other hand, Vicos may have provided a useful precedent in the way of an organizational model. While the Vicos project was based upon a *convenio* (statement of understanding) between the Peruvian Indian Institute and Cornell University, the Kuyo Chico project was based upon a *convenio* between the University of Cuzco and the National Plan for the Integration of the Indian Population, which was an outgrowth of the Indian Institute of the Ministry of Labor and Indian Affairs. The support of Dr. Carlos Monge, President of the Indian Institute, was essential to both projects.

There was also a personal link between Allan Holmberg and Oscar Núñez del Prado. At one time, Núñez del Prado had worked on a research project at Virú on the north coast of Peru, along with other young Peruvian anthropologists, under the direction of Holmberg. The two men came to know each other well and developed a warm relationship and one of mutual respect. On the other hand, the Virú study took place before Holmberg had launched his Vicos project, and we have no record of the two men carrying out any serious discussion regarding specific applied anthropology projects, although, of course, they had ample opportunity to discuss their common interests over a period of several months when they worked together.

Vicos and Kuyo Chico differ in that each one is representative of a different structural type of rural social organization in Peru. Vicos involved an *hacienda* where, typical of that area in Peru, the Indians lived as serfs, performing work for the *hacendado* (owner or renter of the property) in return for the right to cultivate a small family plot of land in the most undesirable area of the estate and to receive a money payment so small that it could be regarded as a token.

The indigenous community was, in the legal theory, a rural community of people who still retained some of the cultural traits considered to be Indian and who, if they had been able to get their community officially recognized, fell under the protection of what was in this period the Ministry of Labor and Indian Affairs. In practice, these were nearly all communities of small, individual family landholdings, although the grazing lands were often held in common. The communities had a tradition of local self-government and, in legal theory, were independent entities, under the protection of the ministry. In practice, large numbers of these communities have been under the domination of Mestizo political authorities and large landowners, whose power base was in the towns and cities. We thus find that in many cases the inhabitants of indigenous communities were as badly exploited economically as hacienda residents, in spite of the assumed protection of the ministry. In the case of Kuyo Chico, we have a community which was not officially recognized at the beginning of the project but which won such recognition as the project proceeded.

Since haciendas and indigenous communities (officially recognized or not) between them made up the bulk of the rural population in highland Peru, the two cases under comparison provide us with valuable material on the problems of intervention and change throughout the rural highlands, up to the period when the government had become a major source of the introduction of changes.

The cases are similar in that the applied anthropologist had to bring about a change in the power structure in each case, relating the Indians to the dominant Mestizos. They differ in the problems and strategies used, and necessarily so, since the power problem came in different forms in the two types of situations. Holmberg solved the internal problem of power when he rented hacienda Vicos, in the name of Cornell University. In effect, this made Holmberg the hacendado and enabled him to go about changing the relations that had traditionally existed between the hacendado and the Indians at Vicos. Since the Vicos hacendado had previously held the monopoly of power locally, Holmberg, by moving into this role, was able to carry out his change strategy with a good deal of freedom of action. This does not mean that he solved with this one move the power problem at Vicos, because, as Vicos became so obviously successful, it came to be considered a threat to the power structure in the surrounding area. Part of the untold story of the Vicos project involves the maneuvers that were carried out by Holmberg, Carlos Monge, Mario Vázquez, and their associates, to maintain Vicos in existence against the overt and covert hostility of politicians and large landowners in Ancash.

Núñez del Prado also intervened between the Indians and the Mestizo power figures in the area to free the Kuyo Chico Indians for their development efforts, but he could not simply take over the role of the hacendado, because he was acting in a situation where no Mestizo or no group of Mestizos owned and controlled Kuyo Chico but where there was a broad pattern of exploitation by Mestizos. A major point of interest in this account is the strategy whereby Núñez del Prado intervened to change the power structure in Kuyo Chico and the district of Pisaq.

Kuyo Chico in the Context of Social Change and Revolution

Since the time of Vicos and Kuyo Chico projects, the political scene has changed drastically in Peru. At the time these projects were begun, Peru was under governments which had no plans to develop rural Peru through fundamental changes in the social, economic, and political structure. Since the military came to power in October of 1968, Peru has been under a government which claims to be carrying out a genuine revolution. Many Peruvians therefore naturally ask whether the lessons of intervention projects in small communities have any meaning in this new era.

We must put such intervention efforts in the broader context of the types of social and economic changes that occur in a country such as Peru. Here again a threefold classification seems useful.

Peasant movements. Many students of social change have been misled in the past by what I call "the myth of the passive peasant": the notion that peasants are by nature tradition-bound, fatalistic, and resistant to change.[2] In this logic, where there is no large-scale government intervention, change can come to the countryside only through the actions of individual change agents who come from the dynamic urban centers.

Our research suggests an opposite view of Peruvian peasants: they are engaged in an active struggle to improve their conditions of life. The visibility of this struggle to outsiders depends in part upon the presence or absence of violence and upon the success or failure of peasant efforts.

Peru has had a long history of peasant movements and rebellions, from efforts on individual haciendas to broader regional efforts. Until about 1950, the repression of peasant militancy was so universally successful that only the more widespread and spectacular peasant efforts attracted much attention on the part of intellectuals and social scientists.

Around the middle of this century, conditions changed in ways that we do not yet fully understand. Peasants continued their struggle, but now they began to win the battles. The first formal protest (*reclamo*) from the peasants of the Convención Valley was filed with the Cuzco office of the Ministry of Labor and Indian Affairs in 1952.[3] Ten years later the government of Peru recognized the expulsion of the hacendados and the assumption of peasant control in this valley of over sixty thousand inhabitants. Furthermore, the peasant movement spilled over into other parts of the department of Cuzco. Chawaytirí, an hacienda next door to Kuyo Chico, was organized into a union in an extension of the Convención Valley movement.

The peasant movement in the Yanamarca Valley of the central sierra began also in the early 1950s, and within about

2. See W. F. Whyte, "Rural Peru—Peasants as Activists," *Trans-Action* 7, no. 1 (November 1969).

3. For a discussion of the Convención Valley transformation, see the Cornell University Ph.D. thesis of Wesley Craig, "From Hacienda to Community: An Analysis of Solidarity and Social Change in Peru," Latin American Studies Program Dissertation Series, no. 6, September 1967.

a decade the peasants had succeeded in transforming five haciendas into independent communities.[4] Similar changes were taking place elsewhere in the highlands during this same period.

In the early days of the Vicos and Kuyo Chico projects, it was reasonable to believe that, since the government was not going to launch a strong rural reform program, intervention efforts provided the anthropologist the only possible opportunity to examine the process of structural transformation of communities and haciendas. In other words, only by generating such changes himself would the anthropologist have the opportunity to study them.

We now see that there was another alternative beyond the applied anthropology project or the government reform program: the peasants might successfully organize themselves. But this conclusion has become clear only through hindsight. While the two peasant movements best known to us through research were indeed under way around the time of the launching of the applied anthropology projects, there was no way of telling at the time that these movements were going to break the pattern of failure in peasant militancy up to 1950. It is only toward the end of the decade of the 1960s that, recognizing the success of several peasant movements, we began concentrating research efforts upon this important route to social change in rural Peru.

Applied anthropology projects. Can interventions in such small communities provide the base for spreading social and economic changes more widely through rural society?

This was the hope of Allan Holmberg and of those Peruvians who worked most closely with him at Vicos. A research and development approach to change would have defined Vicos as a pilot project, testing tactics and strategies of rural

4. For a discussion of the Yanamarca Valley transformation, see the Cornell Ph.D. thesis of Giorgio Alberti, "Inter-village Systems and Development: A Study of Social Change in Highland Peru," Latin American Studies Program Dissertation Series, no. 18, June 1970. For an interpretation of the Yanamarca and Convención cases, see W. F. Whyte, "Rural Peru—Peasants as Activists."

development. On this basis, when it seemed that Vicos had become an economically viable self-governing community, the logical next step would have been to apply the lessons learned at Vicos in a half-dozen other communities or haciendas. On the basis of examining the problems and processes of change in these new projects, the government could then have gone on to devise the strategy and tactics necessary to carry out the structural transformation of large areas of rural Peru.

In fact, during the years immediately after the launching of Vicos, the government did sponsor other projects, such as Puno-Tambopata (with the I.L.O.), Cangallo, Junín, and Kuyo Chico. But these initiatives were taken before it was possible to examine the results of Vicos and profit from that experience. The goverment of President Manuel Prado (1956–62) did indeed plan later projects designed to utilize the lessons of Vicos, but these projects were lost in budget cuts.

Budget cutting always involves a weighing of priorities. In this case, there is reason to believe that key officials of the Peruvian government decided that the extension of the rural experimental program was not only too expensive but was positively undesirable. This interpretation is supported by the great difficulty that the sponsors of the Vicos project experienced in getting the hacienda finally expropriated in favor of its Indian inhabitants. The principal collaborators on the project from the beginning had sought a government commitment to expropriate Vicos within five years, and in fact the government did issue a decree to this effect in 1956. But it was not until mid-1962, in the last days of the Prado regime, that the government carried out its pledge, as a final step in a still unprinted story of maneuvers by proponents and opponents of Vicos.

During the period 1956–62, in nearly every annual report to Congress, President Prado devoted several paragraphs to Vicos, always describing the project in most friendly terms but never indicating any commitment to apply the potential lessons of Vicos on a broader scale. From this we get the impression that the president and his key officials were happy to show off Vicos to the nation and to foreign observers, as an indication of their interest in reform and development, but that they felt it best to have Vicos in a sort of glass case for public relations purposes and not to push any broader programs. It is significant that the expropriation of Vicos proved to be an especially awkward commitment for the government then in power. A key official of this government at one time said privately that he would never approve the expropriation of Vicos because "it would set a terrible precedent." In other words, if Vicos were expropriated, by the same logic, many other haciendas could be turned over to their Indian inhabitants, and the whole social and economic structure of rural Peru would be threatened.

The same general point can be made regarding the Kuyo Chico project. A government really committed to agrarian reform and rural development could have set up an organization to analyze the problems and processes of change involved in Kuyo Chico so as to design a new series of projects, and later, on the basis of the experience of those projects, move on toward a broad-scale program of structural transformation. Of course, nothing of the sort happened. While President Fernando Belaúnde Terry (1963–68) seemed much more inclined than Manuel Prado to push for rural change and development, he was unable to overcome an opposition majority in Congress, which limited his change efforts to community development programs, spearheaded by his "Popular Cooperation" agency. In the political climate then prevailing, the extension of the Kuyo Chico ideas to other areas was out of the question. Supporters of the Kuyo Chico project had all they could do to keep the project in existence; it was financed on a precarious basis, never with the kind of long-range assurance of support that would have made it possible to capitalize upon the lessons of the project.

If the Vicos and Kuyo Chico projects had been followed up by widened efforts to apply what had been learned in these small communities, then, when a government with a commitment to change the basic social and economic structure of the country came to power, it could have built effectively upon the second-stage experiences growing out of the small proj-ects. Furthermore, such a government would have had a much larger cadre of trained and experienced change agents at its disposal for carrying out its revolutionary program at the grass-roots level. This did not happen, and we must conclude that the failure of governmental follow-up was not acci-dental. In other words, neither Vicos nor Kuyo Chico can realistically be considered as preliminary stages of a broad program of structural transformation of rural Peru. In the political climate prevailing as these projects developed, it simply was not possible to extend what was being learned at the hacienda and community level to broader areas. The most we can say is that both projects contributed to the in-tellectual and political ferment concerning agrarian reform.[5]

Oscar Núñez del Prado never advocated projects like Kuyo Chico as a substitute for agrarian reform—nor did Allan Holmberg. When I asked Núñez del Prado whether, if he had financial support, he would want to attempt another project like Kuyo Chico, he shook his head and replied, "Kuyo Chico belonged to one epoch. We are now in a different epoch." We shall now consider the relevance of Kuyo Chico to the new epoch of major governmental intervention in the countryside.

Agrarian reform and structural transformation. Since June of 1969, the military government of Peru has been carrying out an ambitious and comprehensive program of structural transformation in the countryside. The great commercial sugar plantations on the coast have been expropriated from their former owners, and the government is seeking to transform them into producers' cooperatives. In much of highland Peru, the semifeudal haciendas are being turned into peasant com-

5. Henry F. Dobyns sees stronger influences: "the reality of the Indian integration programs that demonstrated that Indians were hu-man, could learn rapidly, and that the difficulties of production and so-cial integration were matters of social structure rather than genes provided fundamental underpinning for the whole political discussion. Many today would like to forget just how prejudiced and discrimina-tory the dominant group was before October of 1968. In the language of Latin American historiography, Vicos and Kuyo Chico should be recognized as *precursores* of present agrarian reform."

munities, with some combination of private-family ownership and cooperative organization. In this process, large landowning families have been losing much of their political power and economic leverage.

When such dramatic changes are taking place at the top of the rural power structure, there is a natural tendency to assume that anything learned in a small Indian community or hacienda would no longer have any practical utility.

Those who take this view overlook the pitfalls that can arise when policy makers concentrate only on "the big picture." Changes made at the top of the power structure do not automatically lead to the desired state of affairs at the grassroots level. At worst, the peasants could simply find that a new set of bosses had been substituted for the old ones. To be sure, the government is firmly committed to an ideology of participation and is trying to devise ways in which workers and peasants can exercise increasing control over their own destinies, but this is an enormously difficult and complicated task. It is not achieved simply through seizing control of organizations and communities.

A change in the power structure is a necessary but not a sufficient condition for creating the new participatory society. Within the new framework of power relations, government policy-makers and administrators need to understand the continuing patterns of the culture of communities and the dynamics of groups and intergroup relations. It is at this microlevel that policies and procedures yield outcomes in peasant behavior and satisfactions. *And it is at this level that the Kuyo Chico case is especially relevant to the policy-makers and administrators of agrarian reform. The noble aims of agrarian reform may be frustrated unless the implementors of the program can understand culture and social processes in communities such as Kuyo Chico.*

Whether as a landmark in the history of applied anthropology or as a contribution to social change in Peru, Kuyo Chico continues to offer some very important values.

1. Nuñez del Prado provides us with one of the most systematic descriptions and analyses of Mestizo-Indian relations

in the sierra that has so far appeared. He translates the epithet of "exploitation" into concrete behavioral and economic terms.

2. The author gives a step-by-step account of the introduction of community changes in housing, farming, health, education, and political organization. He also shows how activities in one sector of community life grow out of and lead to activities in other sectors.

3. The author shows us how changes in power relations open the way to new and more productive group activities in the community.

4. Development efforts often break down when change agents representing different specialties (agriculture, education, health) compete with each other, to the confusion and frustration of the peasants. The author shows us a team approach to development.

5. The book links together measures of changes in attitudes and beliefs with a description of the behavior that brought about such changes.

Knowledge on all five of these points should be of value both to students of social change and to change agents involved in development programs.

KUYO CHICO

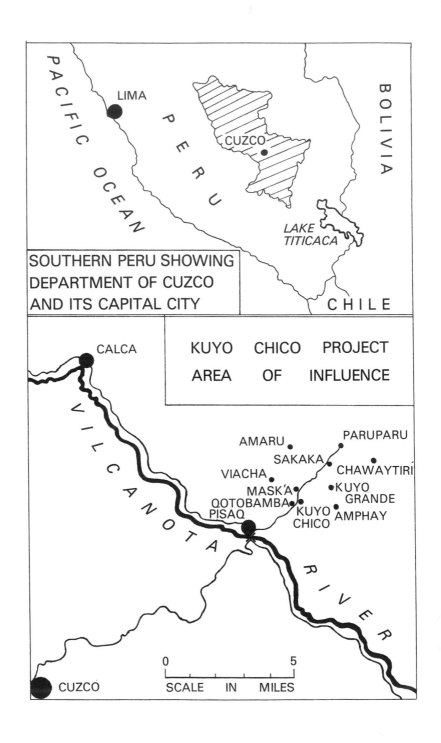

SOUTHERN PERU SHOWING
DEPARTMENT OF CUZCO
AND ITS CAPITAL CITY

PACIFIC OCEAN

LIMA

P E R U

CUZCO

BOLIVIA

LAKE
TITICACA

C H I L E

KUYO   CHICO   PROJECT
AREA   OF   INFLUENCE

CALCA

V I L C A N O T A

AMARU

SAKAKA

PARUPARU

CHAWAYTIRÍ

VIACHA

MASK'A

KUYO
GRANDE

QOTOBAMBA

PISAQ

KUYO
CHICO

AMPHAY

R I V E R

CUZCO

0   5
SCALE   IN   MILES

1
Preparing for Intervention

The history of this program begins in 1955 when, under the direction of the author, the National University of Cuzco sent an anthropological expedition to the region of Q'ero, under the auspices of the Lima newspaper *La Prensa*.

Q'ero was one of the most isolated regions of Peru and was made up of eight subsections: Totorani, Kiko, Hapu, K'allakancha, Pukara, Markachea, Q'achupata, and Q'ero proper. It was located in a vast mountainous region with a scattered population of more than five thousand Indians, who were subject to an hacienda system which involves the exchange of labor for the use of land. The required labor could range from care of the crops; *pongueaje*, or domestic service in the household of the *patrón; sétimas,* or turns at shepherding (with full responsibility for the herds); turns as *pisqero,* or watchman in the gardens of the patrón; to the *mita* services which were abolished by Bolívar in 1824. These services were still preserved in Q'ero in two forms: groups of peons could be sent to the landowner's other haciendas, 92 kilometers away, or they could be rented out to other haciendas in the Urubamba Valley, in which case they received one-fifth of a Peruvian *sol* (the *sol* then equaled about 4 cents) for their subsistence, while the patrón received the salary which by law the other hacendado must pay them. In addition, the established system involved a series of extra labors which were required of the *peasant* but did not result in any additional benefits for him, and which consisted of whatever the patrón wanted done. In all, the labor required represented between 180 and 250 days of work a year, exclusively for the benefit of the landowner, to the point that the laborer found it impossible to work his own land. As a result, his wife and children had to take responsibility for the family's herd and crops.

This large burden of duties and obligations had been accepted without opposition by the Indians. Lacking a clear understanding of their rights, they had developed forms of essentially fatalistic thinking which justified their situation. They believed that the world order is based upon inequalities which originated by divine will (*la voluntad divina*), and thus that it was fruitless and impossible to question the established order. Nevertheless, there was also a profound belief that the possibility of advancement is connected with the ability to read and write Spanish. Some had tried to send their children to schools in other areas, but such audacity had been smothered by the hacendado through the expulsion of these families. In general, there was an eagerness to learn new things which was expressed in the belief that a large part of their situation was due to the fact that they were "blind" (illiterate).

This situation made us think that it was essential to obtain the expropriation of this hacienda before establishing a program to work towards improving the living conditions of the Indians. First a series of charges was made before the Peruvian Indian Institute, demanding the abolition of the established systems of free labor. Through these first actions, the general secretary of the Institute, Dr. Manuel Velasco Nuñez, obtained a series of directives from the Ministry of Labor and Indian Affairs which put an end to these various forms of servitude.

We then entered into closer contact with the Indian Institute, and in mid-1958 they dispatched an anthropologist, Mario Vázquez Varela (of Project Vicos), and an engineer, Hugo Contreras Quevedo, to Q'ero. We returned with them to complete some studies, and it was with Vázquez that we formulated our first plan for a program of applied anthropological studies in Q'ero, which met with the approval of Dr. Velasco Núñez.

The attempts to obtain an appropriation from the Ministry of Labor and Indian Affairs were progressing well, to the point that the Indian Institute decided to go ahead with the program. Dr. Sergio Quevedo Aragón, anthropologist and rector of the University of Cuzco, supported the plan, and on March 17, 1959, signed an agreement between the university and the Institute to begin the work in Q'ero. However, despite the fact that we had started proceedings to obtain the expropriation of the hacienda well ahead of time, the hacendado did all in his power to impede us, and it became impossible to start our project.

Through a new agreement between the university and the Institute, it was decided to proceed with the program in a different region of Cuzco. In April, at the suggestion of the university, the Institute designated me the director of the program, later adding Hugo Contreras, agricultural engineer, and Rodolfo Sánchez C., educator. We were to select a community in Cuzco for the project, and for this purpose we surveyed the provinces of Quispicanchis, Canchis, Espinar, Canas, Anta, Urubamba, and Calca. In June we arrived at Pisaq, capital of one of the districts of Calca, where we contacted Dr. Felipe Marín, a university professor who has a small estate in that area. He suggested that we go to the village of Kuyo Chico, and offered to accompany us.

On our way to the village, we came upon a man carrying wood on his back. Marín told us that this was Tomás Díaz Qhapa, *cabecilla* of Kuyo Chico.[1] We stopped to converse with him and expressed our desire to help his community attain better living conditions. Don Tomás seemed quite terrified, but was sufficiently cordial to give us some important information. He told us that the road which passed through Kuyo Chico, a very old dirt road, united the district of Pisaq with the capital of the province of Paucartambo, and that

---

1. Local official (head of the community) appointed by the governor of Pisaq. See below, "Community Government," in chapter 2.

1. Approach to Kuyo Chico with old houses and remodeled
house in background

along its length were a series of Indian communities. Kuyo
Chico was one of the poorest communities in the area as well
as one of the smallest, having a total of about one hundred
hectares of land, most of it uncultivable.[2] Don Tomás explained that they had lost their best lands when a neighboring
hacendado, after obtaining a court order to expel them, kicked
them off and burned their homes. He also told us of the extreme poverty in Kuyo Chico, and of the abuses which the
Indians suffered at the hands of the Mestizos. When we arrived at Kuyo Chico, Don Tomás introduced us to other members of the community, and after conversing with them, we
came to the conclusion that although they were very timid,
they were inclined to be communicative.

2. One hectare equals 2.47 acres.

It appeared to us that Kuyo Chico was a very good community in which to start our program. We had not really expected to find a place where it would be easy to proceed with our work, and because this village was extremely poor, it seemed to us that in the future the surrounding communities would be able to observe quite clearly whatever changes had been brought about by our program. Thus we decided to locate the center of our operations in Kuyo Chico, and communicated this decision to the university, which, under the terms of the agreement, was represented by a committee of anthropologists. The president of this committee was Dr. Sergio Quevedo Aragón, rector of the University. Through a conference with the Indian Institute, it was decided that Kuyo Chico would be a kind of pilot project for a program applying anthropology to the problems of integration of an Indian community. The Institute, directed by Dr. Carlos Monge Medrano, was represented by a technical committee headed by its general secretary, Dr. Manuel D. Velasco Núñez.

In accordance with the framework formulated by the Institute, the following personnel were selected for the program, upon the recommendation of the university.

Director, Social Anthropologist—Dr. Oscar Núñez del Prado
Physical Anthropologist—Dr. Sergio Quevedo Aragón
Agricultural Engineer—Hugo Contreras Quevedo
Educator—Prof. Rodolfo Sánchez C.
Doctor—Dr. Rigoberto Dávila A.
Teacher of Home Economics—Mrs. Estela Perea
Administrator—Juan Gonzáles Iberico
Chauffeur—Angel Noriega Seiner

The size of the staff was shortly reduced and continued to vary greatly from that point on, with the positions of director (social anthropologist), educator, administrator, and chauffeur being the most stable.

In June of the same year, the Committee of Anthropologists was dissolved, and several months later the National Plan for

Integration of the Indian Population (*Plan Nacional de Integración de la Población Aborigen*) was instituted, under the direction of Dr. Pelegrín Román Unzueta, who assumed responsibility for all the programs which had been under the direction of the Indian Institute. This arrangement continued until 1965, when the Institute resumed its function, still directed by Dr. Román. With the Committee dissolved, Dr. Núñez del Prado remained director of the program, maintaining relations with the executive office of the Plan for Integration and assuming responsibility for the orientation and execution of the work. Thus the Plan for Integration and the Institute paid expenses and handled administration, while the University of Cuzco, through the director it designated, was responsible for executing the program.

An agreement had been signed to carry out a program of applied anthropology toward the integration of the Indian community, but the terms of the agreement had not been concretely defined by the Institute. Integration was spoken of as "necessary," but it was not clear what this meant. The question was left to those of us operating in the field to resolve, upon full consideration of all the issues involved. If we speak of a national process of integration, should we think merely in terms of acculturation? Should we seek the full absorption of the dominated culture by the dominating culture without taking into account the usefulness and validity of elements found in the former? The present Indian culture maintains remnants of traditional institutions which we considered important to conserve. In addition, there are aspects of the Westernized Mestizo culture which facilitate men's efforts to provide for the necessities of life. Should we, then, seek to integrate these elements of existing systems in both cultures which are of the greatest value to men in the solution of their problems?

We do not believe that integration is merely a simple transfer of elements. National integration will be the result of taking the best aspects of both cultures and forming a homogeneous species of a third order. The aim of integration is to achieve a balanced fusion of the positive features of both cultures while eliminating the negative features. The validity of such traditional institutions as the *ayni* and the family in rural agricultural life cannot be denied, but to equalize the participation of the Indian in national life, these aspects of the Indian culture must be united with the technological resources of the Mestizo culture.

We must remember, however, that since the process of integration signifies a step towards new forms and conditions of life, it must proceed gradually, so as not to produce the dislocation and anxiety which come from rapid and disorderly social change. The case of the *Cholo* in Peru provides an example of such anguish and insecurity, for he is constantly tormented by the uncertainty of his relationship to the patrón, and fluctuates between the Mestizo and Indian cultures while belonging to neither.[3]

In accord with these ideas, we believed that, in order to fulfill our goals, it was important to make an anthropological study of the relations which the communities had with each other and with the capital of the district, within the general context of the predominant culture of the area. Only this broad vision of the whole, coupled with more detailed knowledge of the particular community chosen for the study, would permit us to establish our center of operations and carry out our program. Without a profound understanding of the many threads in the complex weave of the culture, the motives and conduct of the Indians would have remained illogical and inexplicable from our point of view. Only on the basis of such knowledge could we formulate a valid course of action.

Here we must emphasize the importance of the meaning which things have in the Indian culture, of the ideas and beliefs which permeate and tie together the various activities of daily life in the communities. We believe that it is these meanings, these forms of thinking and the activities bound to them, which constitute the determinants of individual and collective attitudes and behavior. Consequently, an understanding of the culture was the only thing which could pro-

3. The Cholo will be more fully defined in the next chapter.

vide us with the criteria necessary to determine which would be the most appropriate and effective courses of action to follow in order to bring about changes in the opinions, attitudes, and actions of the group. If the ideas and programs which we introduced were related to already existing meanings in the culture, rather than based solely on our own point of view, the receptivity of the group would be greatest, since those "innovations" would be in accord with the group's own modes of thought. Acceptance of new concepts, techniques, and habits would be smoothest and most rapid. Furthermore, by proceeding in this manner, we would attain the greatest level of participation from the group.

2

Kuyo Chico and Its Microregion

Social Groups

Throughout this work we will speak of two sociocultural groups: the Mestizos and the Indians, or peasants. This perspective is based on the manner in which the Indian perceives his own situation. However, it will be helpful, particularly in some of the cases which we will discuss, to characterize the situation in terms of four social groups rather than two.

The Indian occupies the lowest level on the social scale. He is generally an agricultural worker and lives in the country, either in a community or on an hacienda. He is monolingual in Quechua, illiterate, and doesn't vote in the general elections. He dresses in what are called "typical" clothes of the region: rough, homemade woolens, knitted caps (ch'ullus), and brightly colored ponchos. He goes barefoot or wears sandals made from automobile tires, and on special occasions wears a round ceremonial hat (montera). He provides for himself most of the necessities of subsistence, chews the coca leaf, and is subject to pressures from all the other social groups. Politically, he can aspire to be cabecilla of his community, mayor of the staff (alcalde de vara),[1] jefe de banda,[2] or school deputy (teniente escolar).[3]

1. Mayor of a larger Indian community.
2. Neighborhood leader or representative. Communities are divided into subsections (bandas) along neighborhood or family lines. See section on "Community Government" in this chapter.
3. Selected by the director of the school and hired as administrative

Chapter Two

The *Cholo* is an Indian who has left the community or hacienda to live in the town, working at a trade or craft (carpentry, ironwork, masonry) or in small commerce. He may be employed as a butler or foreman on an hacienda, or serve as an *alcanzador*.[4] He speaks Spanish as well as Quechua, his mother tongue, and generally has a military or electoral identification book which allows him to vote in the national elections. These symbols are crucial for active participation in national life. He normally dresses in manufactured cottons, wearing a poncho of beige or gray and usually wearing sandals rather than shoes. He generally has completed the third grade of primary school education, and can aspire to some lower-level public offices, such as *teniente gobernador*,[5] or municipal agent, who is responsible to the mayor for a section of the municipality. He gets drunk frequently, and, if he chews coca, tries to hide this fact. He looks down on the Indian and tries to demonstrate that he is far superior to him; he dislikes it if people who are not Indian speak to him in Quechua. He is constantly preoccupied with trying to hide his Indian extraction.

The *Mozo* is a transitional class between the *Cholo* and the Mestizo proper. He lives in the town, though not in central neighborhoods, and is involved in various types of business. He may be a barterer, *alcanzador,* shepherd, or trucker, or a journeyman in such trades as carpentry, tailoring, ironwork, and shoemaking. He is a small landowner employing agricultural workers (*peones*). He speaks, reads, and writes Spanish, using Quechua in the intimacy of his family life and in dealings with the Indians. He wears manufactured clothing of an old-fashioned cut, high-laced shoes, and a cloth hat. He has eliminated the poncho from his daily wardrobe, reserving it for travel or rainy weather. He generally has completed grade school, and may become a public official, such as district governor, assistant to the justice of the peace, or secre-

---

aide. Actual duties range from taking attendance to cleaning the school and running errands for school officials.

4. See "Indian-Mestizo Relations" in this chapter.

5. Lieutenant governor: the lowest level of provincial official.

tary to the municipal council. He is very dynamic, generally belongs to some political party, and votes regularly in the elections.

The Mestizo proper occupies the position at the top of the social scale. He is a landowner, businessman, or public official. He controls his own affairs and has underlings at his disposal; if he owns land, he directs the agriculture on them. His house is large and located in the center of town, and he wears the latest styles in clothing. His relations with the capitals of the province and department are intense, and he participates actively in politics, occupying such positions as justice of the peace, governor, school teacher, municipal mayor, or preeminent member of the municipal council. He sends his children to secondary schools or centers of higher education in the cities, and his ties with people in the city and in higher spheres of politics afford him much power and influence in the town. His habitual language is Spanish, but he speaks Quechua and uses it in his relations with the Indians, or when he wants to humiliate the *Mozo* or *Cholo*.

These three social groups, the *Cholos,* the *Mozos,* and the Mestizos proper, we group together as "Mestizos," because of their common interests and orientation. The Indian views the Cholo as belonging to the Mestizo group, and the Cholo identifies himself with the Mestizo rather than with the Indian.

Power

Power is in the hands of the Mestizos of Pisaq, who constitute one of the lower levels in a hierarchical power structure centered in Cuzco, the capital city of the department. Political power increases as one moves up the levels in the pyramid. Local authorities are subordinate to the authorities in the provincial capital, who in turn are subordinate to the higher authorities in the department capital; thus the controls of the system are centered in Cuzco. However, we must remember that the greatest power, in terms of influence and control over individuals, is exercised by the authorities at one level over their immediate inferiors at the next lowest level. The direct control which officials exercise over their inferiors diminishes as the two groups move farther apart in the scale; as one ascends in the power structure, his actual contact with and influence upon the lives of the people lessens. In this manner, the influence of the higher authorities, such as the prefect of Cuzco or the subprefect of Calca, is not as direct as that of the lower authorities, such as the governors and lieutenant governors of the districts, and the greatest power over the daily lives of the Indians in this area is exercised by the Mestizo authorities of Pisaq, who use the local Indian officials (cabecillas, envarados, segundas) as instruments to carry out their commands.

Local Administration of Justice

The judicial system is organized nationally, with centralization, uniform judicial structures at all levels, and judicial procedures prescribed by law. A justice of the peace and his assistants carry out the judicial function at the local level. Local political authorities, such as the governor, lieutenant governor, police chief, and even the municipal officials, enforce the decisions of the local courts, as well as those of the various superior courts. At the provincial level, an Inspección de Asuntos Indígenas (Indian Affairs Office) concerned with administrative and judicial matters involving Indians used to function from Cuzco.

At the local level political officials went beyond the legal limits of their authority, as prescribed in the formal system of justice, and assumed a decision-making role as well as one of enforcement. Both they and the local judicial authorities displayed a great deal of favoritism in their decisions, which were influenced by the social class of the litigants, their economic situation, or their social ties with the authorities. Because these officials always expected to gain some benefit from a person involved or implicated in a case, it can be said that decisions were based on the way in which one supported economically those who made them. This attitude of expecting personal gain was due, in large part, to the fact that, with the exception of the police, the authorities in question were not paid by the state. The governor, lieutenant governor, mayor, and justices of the peace all had regular employment or professions in addition to their government posts. These posts provided sizable supplementary incomes. Since there was no regulation of the rates charged for their services, they charged in accord with the opportunities presented to them. When we arrived in the area, they were charging arbitrarily for personal inspections of problems, assessments, judicial dispositions which they received from higher courts, and so on. In strictly local cases involving concrete issues, the justices of the peace charged for contracts, records of transactions or agreements, and records of civil decisions, exacting money or personal services from the litigants. Even at the provincial level, a person who had been held in jail or needed some service would be required to do work in the homes of the authorities—if he was an Indian.

This system of arbitrary charges was supposed to be eliminated by a law requiring the giving of receipts, with the receipt books controlled by higher authorities. However, the law was not adhered to, and the arbitrary charges continued.

Community Government

Indian authorities have local jurisdiction over the communities, the precise structure of the governing system varying at this level according to the size of the community and its distance from the capital of the district. Small communities, such as Qotobamba, Mask'a, Kuyo Chico, and Qotataki, each had a *cabecilla* designated by the governor of Pisaq. Other communities, such as Kuyo Grande, Amaru, Paru-Paru, and Sakaka, located in higher regions farther from the capital, encompassing greater areas and more inhabitants, were governed by *alcaldes envarados*.[6] In this system, the mayor

6. A traditional title, not legally recognized.

(*alcalde*) sits at the head of the community's governing body, which is made up of his subordinates: *segundas, regidores, alguaciles*. When a community is very large, there are also auxiliary authorities, the *delegados de banda* (*jefes de banda*), who are elected representatives of each of the subsections of the community (*bandas*), which is divided along neighborhood or family lines.

The situation of these Indian authorities contrasts greatly with that of the powerful Mestizo authorities. For example, theoretically a mayor is elected by the community, and he in turn designates the *segundas, regidores,* and *alguaciles*. However, the mayor-elect can be vetoed by the governor of the district if he is considered unfit for the job, and generally the members of the community receive indications from the governor before the elections designating the possible candidates. The granting of the staff (*vara*) as a symbol of authority is made by the governor in an annual ceremony held in January.

In general, the community authorities (*cabecillas, envarados*) are absolutely subordinate to the Mestizo authorities. Beyond intervening to arbitrate in small disputes, complaints, or damages occasioned by animals in the farm plots (*chacras*), the function of the community authorities is limited to being mere executors of the dispositions and decisions of the Mestizos. These authorities notify the people of the levy of peonage (exacted by the capital of the district), confiscate household objects as security to force the people to go to the work duties (*faenas*) imposed by the mestizos, and take the required "offerings" of lambs to the authorities (*los carneros de las turnas*). In short, they perform the odious function of pressuring their community into a series of contributions and services for the benefit of the Mestizos.

Indian-Mestizo Relations

The relations of the Indians to the Mestizos throughout this valley are represented by the manner in which the authorities use the Indians in various ways to benefit the other Mestizos in the town, who have come to believe that they have a series of rights over the Indians simply by virtue of being Mestizos. For example, local authorities call *faenas* for "public works," justifying this act by declaring that the Indian lives on state lands (the community) but doesn't contribute to the treasury. By means of the whip, the extraction of goods, or the threat of jail, they force the Indians of the communities to go into town, where instead of being employed in public works, they are assigned to a series of private jobs for the benefit of the Mestizos. Thus they not only sweep the streets of the town, but the private homes of the Mestizos as well. They may also be assigned to agricultural work, building of private homes, or carrying of firewood. Similarly, a system of *muy-muy,* or turns, was established, by which the Indian authorities were obliged weekly to take a lamb to each of the Mestizo authorities (the governor, mayor, parson, justice of the peace, and so on). Furthermore, in the event of a visit to Pisaq by an important official, such as a politician or educational authority, the Mestizos would arrange a welcoming reception in the town. Commissions would be sent to the communities to invade the homes of the Indians and seize their small animals, such as guinea pigs, chickens, pigs, and sheep, which were simply "appropriated" for the purposes of the reception.

These relations with the authorities are typical of the general nature of Indian-Mestizo relations in the area, since any Mestizo who has the opportunity to do so will take advantage of the Indian, who in turn puts himself into situations in which he will be exploited.

Each Sunday, the Indians go to the fair in Pisaq to sell their products and purchase their provisions. On the way from their community to the town, they encounter Mestizo *alcanzadores* (mostly Mozo or Cholo), who post themselves along the route and detain the Indians in order to "purchase" their products. They take the merchandise that they want from the Indians and "bargain" to lower prices, generally paying 45–50 percent of what the products are worth at the Pisaq market.

In the town itself, whether by explicit or tacit agreement

among the storeowners, there had been established a barter system of exploitation. According to this arrangement, the Indians cannot purchase basic necessities such as salt and kerosene with money, but are obliged to turn over certain products (eggs, cheese, milk, potatoes—sometimes personal labor) in exchange for these articles. In this form of barter, the Indian loses in two ways: first, he receives a smaller amount of the article purchased than he is entitled to, and, second, he is given a very poor price for the products he offers in exchange. For example, if eggs are sold for ninety centavos each at the market in Cuzco, the Indian will be paid twenty centavos, receiving twelve ounces of salt in return rather than a full pound.

There are two types of Mestizo buyers who go into the communities to do their business, usually in the "high" communities more distant from the town. One type, generally Cholo, brings such articles as coca, salt, *aji* (red pepper), bread, and cigarettes to exchange for Indian products, while the other, generally Mozo, brings money which he gives to the Indians as a forced advance on their harvests. The Indians are constantly obliged to accept such advances without soliciting or desiring them, and in this way are obligated to turn over their products at a 50 percent loss at harvest time. For example, the buyer of sheep and pigs will come and choose the best animals from the herd, leaving the Indian a sum of money which often does not even approach half their worth. We have intervened in cases where an Indian was receiving 10 or 20 *soles* for sheep worth 100 to 120 *soles*. Often people from outside the area exploited the Indians in the same way as the Mestizos of the town, as in the case of a teacher who received an interim appointment to one of the communities, collected a small herd of sheep while there, and took them with him at the conclusion of his appointment.

Relationships between the *colonos* and the patrón on an hacienda follow similar patterns. According to the system of *waki,* the landowner gives use of his land to the Indian, who must work it with his own tools, seeds, and labor, and is then obliged to turn over half of his harvest to the hacendado. In many cases the Indian is "persuaded" to sell his products at reduced prices to the patrón.

Enganchadores are Mestizo agents who get peons for the haciendas in the tropical zone, where men are needed for hard labor, and women and children for domestic service or collecting coffee and coca. These agents generally work under a system in which they are paid in proportion to the number of peons they provide. Thus having an interest in obtaining the greatest possible number of peons, they use all available methods of persuasion. For example, an enganchador may offer an Indian in the sierra an advance on his salary, using money provided for this purpose by the hacendado, and promise to take him personally to the hacienda or pay his passage to such regions as La Convención, Quincemil, and Q'osñipata. Since life is more expensive and labor less abundant in these areas, salaries are generally much higher than those in Pisaq. The Indians are led to believe that they will receive higher wages if they go to work in these areas, and eventually, with the aid of the justice of the peace in Pisaq are talked into making oral or written contracts, the terms and duration of which they do not understand.

Once on the hacienda, the hacendados tend to keep them, against their will, much longer than the time originally stipulated. Usually they do not pay the promised salaries. Furthermore, as a result of changes in climate, diet, and living and working conditions, as well as the lack of adequate preventive medicine, many of these migrants return to their communities in very poor health, contracting anquilostomiasis, anemia, malaria, and tuberculosis.

Even though there exist laws protecting children and regulating the work of minors, the enganchadores generally make light of them, and arrange for children to leave their homes, often without their parents' knowledge. Since the children may have run away from home before, their parents often have no idea where they can find and reclaim them. In one case, an Indian of Kuyo Grande came to our office for help in reclaiming three children, ranging in age from eight to fourteen. According to inquiries which he had made, they had been fooled by an enganchador whom he knew. We made a claim against the enganchador, and in the police station, when we criticized him for his human commerce, and insinuated that he should dedicate himself to some other business, he replied, "The Indian is the best business and you are spoiling it."

There is also another type of enganchador who obtains young girls between ten and eighteen years of age, ostensibly to work as "maids" in the cities of Cuzco, Arequipa, and Lima. This type of traffic is carried on by Mestizo women who have ties with the city.

Personal Intergroup Relations

The spiritual parentage established through the system of *compadrazgo* (ritual kinship) plays an important role in the relations between the Indians and Mestizos. The force of the rights and obligations established in this way is greater with *Mozos* and *Cholos* than with the Mestizo proper. With the latter, these ties have a more objective character, through concrete acts of lending and returning services, whereas the relation between the *Mozo* and *Cholo* and the Indian has an additional subjective meaning or emotional profundity which makes the obligations of the parties involved much deeper.

There are three principal types of compadrazgo relationships, revolving around marriage, baptism, and the cutting of the first hair. In compadrazgo by marriage, the closest relationship is established between the godchildren and the godparents. Here it is believed that it is desirable to look for godparents who have stable homes and live in harmony and agreement, because these qualities are transferred in some degree to the home which the godchildren will form. The godfather, by so being, contracts the obligation of guiding the relations of the married couple, and among the powers granted to him is the right to impose or inflict by his own hand bodily punishment upon whichever spouse does not behave properly. In addition, he must present and bear the costs of one of the days of fiesta celebrating the marriage, and owes to his godchildren protection against strangers. The godchildren are obliged to be respectful and obedient to their godparents, and to lavish upon them all the work or service that may be solicited.

In *padrinazgo* by baptism, the principal relationship is established between the godparents and the parents of the child—the *compadrazgo* relation. The godparents are obligated to provide the baptism gown and pay the priests and sacristans involved in the ceremony (and, in the event of the death of the child, to bear the costs of the burial clothes and the coffin, and part of the burial expenses). Nevertheless, other obligations to the godchildren become lesser in time, and those established with the compadres remain most tangible. The godfather is morally obligated to provide protection and help for the parents, which is sometimes translated into small gifts. The father is obligated to lend his services as they are required by the godfather, and to visit him, bringing a gift, with some frequency.

The cutting of the first hair has greater significance when the *compadrazgo* relationship is established between Indians, rather than between Indian and Mestizo. In this case the godfather (*padrino*) is obligated to make a considerable gift, often equivalent to constituting the godchild as his sole heir if he has no children of his own. For this reason, it is with great difficulty that the typical Indian accepts being godfather for the cutting of the first hair. On the other hand, when this relationship is established between Indian and Mestizo, it has a highly concrete content. The principal godparent, who is designated to cut the longest braid, is only obligated to make a present, of animals or money, which is greater than the gifts given by the other godparents, who cut the secondary braids.

The Indian tends to try to relate himself to the Mestizo by way of the first two types of godparenthood, looking for godparents who boast of much power and influence, for the real function of these relationships is to obtain some security through the protection which the Mestizo compadre can provide, whether with respect to Mestizos or to other Indians. Protection from other Mestizos remains slight, however, because of their own relationships and power, but nevertheless it is true that often the Mestizo compadre can neutralize or at least lessen the pressure exerted on the Indian. With regard to other Indians, the security he can provide is evident; for example, he can use his power to decide favorably when his compadre has differences with other Indians.

In general, it can be said that the relationships of god-parenthood decrease the possibility of a generalized exploitation of the Indian by channeling this exploitation into the hands of the Mestizo compadres, who, in protecting the Indian from exploitation by other Mestizos, monopolize his services for themselves. For this reason, the Mestizo always welcomes the opportunity to become compadre to an Indian, since this offers one more way in which to take advantage of him. The Indian, on the other hand, tends to select for his compadre either another Indian, which can provide great emotional satisfaction but offers little protection from other Indians and even less from Mestizos, or a Mestizo for whom he will have to perform many services, but not so many as he would have to perform for other Mestizos if he did not have this compadre to intervene for him.

We have indicated that the Mestizo proper pays little attention to his obligations to an Indian compadre, perhaps because to him this relationship offers only an opportunity for personal gain. Among the Mozo and Cholo sectors, however, there exists in addition to this perspective of self-interest a set of beliefs giving a religious meaning to the compadrazgo relationship. Hence these relationships have a deeper psychological and emotional meaning for the Mozo and Cholo, who will be more concerned than the Mestizo with fulfilling their sacred duties, among which is the protection of their compadres. In selecting a compadre, the Indian looks not only for a powerful man, but also for one who will desire to help him effectively. Though the Mozo has less power than the Mestizo proper, he surpasses him in the firmness of his pledge to protect his compadre. Since he has more power than the Cholo, the greatest proportion of compadrazgo relationships are established between the Mozo and the Indian.

Despite the existence of these types of relationships, there remains a great pressure of separation between the Mestizos and the Indians, rooted in history and informed by the profound distrust which the Indian has of the Mestizo. For centuries, the Mestizo has treated the Indian as a useful object, never recognizing his most elementary rights and rarely even stopping to consider him as a human being. The image which the Indian has of the Mestizo is that of an individual with a different physical makeup, composed of elements which produce a type of human being devoid of generous sentiments. He is the individual who only approaches the Indian in order to harass him or make use of him for some personal benefit. As a result, when the Indian has to deal with a Mestizo, he is reticent and distrustful. Though he never shows an openly aggressive attitude, he tries to avoid contact with the Mestizos. This profound separation constitutes an obstacle for the researcher in his attempt to understand the condition of the Indian.

Aspects of the Microeconomy

The principal occupation of the inhabitants of Kuyo Chico is agriculture, through which they obtain, directly or indirectly, the greater part of the necessities of life for a population of about 350. Yet the scarcity of cultivable lands is suffocating. Of a total surface area of 130.75 *topos,* 90.56 percent were dry and only 9.44 percent irrigated.[7] The 35 hectares of land in the community were distributed among 62 families in the following way: from a half to one and a half topos, 34 percent; from two to two and a half topos, 32 percent; from three to four topos, 24.5 percent; from five to seven topos, 7.5 percent; and 1.9 percent without lands. The average amount of land per family was 2.11 topos, or about 1.5 acres, with a per capita average of 0.1 hectares (one-fourth acre). An analysis of the soil composition indicated poor, sandy soil.

7. A topo is a unit of area equalling 2,718 square meters, or about three-fourths of an acre. A hectare equals 10,000 square meters, or 2.47 acres.

An inventory conducted in 1959 gave the following data on the types and quantities of animals, plants, and tools existing in the community.

Animals

cattle (69 cows, 39 bulls, 23 oxen, 23 yearling calves)	154
sheep	74
goats	22
asses	9
pigs	36
mules	2
chickens	160
guinea pigs	377
ducks	2
dogs	46
cats	4

Trees

eucalyptus	387
kiswar	42
peach	20
cherry	18
elder	17
alder	2

Tools and Implements

sickles	105
hoes *(lampas)*	69
plowshares	64
chakitaqllas (pre-Colombian foot-plows)	45
picks	65
adzes	41
pointed hoes *(lampillas)*	36
wooden spades	29
yokes for oxen	11
axes	14
clod-crushers	4
frame saws	3

The lands of the community are used for the following crops:

corn	53.9 percent of total area
wheat	27.5 percent
barley	16.2 percent
peas	1.6 percent
quinua	0.3 percent
beans	0.5 percent

All of the families cultivate corn, as it constitutes a basic part of the regional diet. Ninety-six percent of the people use cattle dung to fertilize their lands; 34 percent add sheep dung, and 3.8 percent complement their fertilizer with ashes.

As secondary occupations in addition to agriculture, 18.9 percent of the people make boards and 52.8 percent firewood, with 41.5 percent buying the trees from neighboring haciendas. The young people also engage in small-scale intercommunity commerce.

The annual calendar of activities revolves around the two great seasons, *poqoy* (the rainy season) and *chirau* (the dry season), within which most of the months are identified with festivals and events in the religious calendar, as follows.

January—New Year and Festival of the Kings. Planting of wheat and barley, plowing, seasonal migration in pursuit of work.

February—Carnival and Festival of Compadres and Comadres. Collection of wood, domestic work, seasonal migration.

March—collection of firewood, weeding of wheat and barley, seasonal migration.

April—Holy Week. Very little work in the community. Weeding of wheat and barley, seasonal migration.

May—Festival of the finding of the True Cross. Hard work. Harvesting of corn, wheat, and beans, cutting and drying of corn.

June—Señor de Qoyllurit'l, celebrated in community of Quispicanchis. Saint Peter and Saint Paul. Hard work. Harvest of barley, wheat, and peas.

July—Patron Santiago and Independence Day. Threshing of wheat and barley, husking of corn.

Chapter Two

September—The Nativity and Festival of Our Lord of Huanca. Celebrated in district of San Salvador. Intense planting of corn, conclusion of threshing of wheat and barley.
October—Last planting of corn and mounding of first planting.
November—All Saints' Day and the Day of the Dead. Intensity of agricultural work diminishes. Mounding of corn, weeding.
December—Christmas. Mounding of corn, planting of wheat in furrows.

The scarcity of cultivable lands confronts the Indian with the problem of providing for his family, which he solves by soliciting the use of lands in the neighboring haciendas, submitting to the conditions imposed by the landowner in exchange for the use of the land. Usually he is obligated to work on the hacienda between 90 and 120 days per year per *topo* of land used, depending on an assessment of the land's quality by the hacendado. Often he does not fulfill his obligation by working on the same hacienda; in some cases Kuyo Indians have had to work on local landowners' haciendas in Anta, La Convención, or the jungle zone of Q'osñipata. If the hacendado requires more days of work than are owed to him, he pays the Indian a symbolic salary which fluctuates between 1.8 and 3.7 U.S. cents per day, in addition to providing the portion of *chicha* to which the Indian is entitled each work day.[8] However, as the cost of this provision has become more inconvenient for the hacendado, a sum of money (20 centavos) is given the peon as compensation for the chicha to which he is entitled.

At the time that we arrived in Kuyo Chico, the average annual income per family did not exceed $67. This amount came from the harvesting of their lands, from wages which the head of the family could obtain (in very few cases amounting to $11 a year), and from small sales by the women of eggs or chicha, or through bartering with the Indians of the high communities.

It should be noted that the microeconomy of Kuyo Chico can be fully understood only within the broader context of

8. A fermented drink made from corn or other grains.

26

the regional economy, the key feature of which is the nature of the economic and social relations between the communities and the district capital. These relations reflect the general character of Indian-Mestizo relationships that we described earlier.

The Family

Although there is a fair degree of social homogeneity in Kuyo Chico, some very subtle differences in the prestige of certain families can be noted. More esteem is accorded to those families whose roots are local and go back very far in the history of the community. The members of these families are referred to as *llaqtayoq* (originating here). The foreign origin of other families, even some which have been in the community for several generations, is not forgotten, and the members of these families are called *quullu* (strange, or foreign). In addition, there are small differences in family prestige which do not relate directly to family history, but perhaps have an economic connotation.

Although the family rests upon a conjugal base of patrilocal residence and reckons descent through the male line, bilateral kin relations are exceedingly extensive and serve as the basis for practically all relations of reciprocity and collaboration.

The male is the head of the family; as such, his authority, in theory, is absolute and final. The other members of the family owe him the deepest respect and should always obey his orders. He does the agricultural work and handles all external relations. As a husband, he assumes the responsibility of supporting his wife and children and is obligated by tradition to put the entire harvest at the disposal of his wife. One part of his responsibilities which is given a special significance is the provision of firewood. This duty seems to be tied to the very concept of the home as the nucleus of all family relations. On one occasion, when a particular couple had decided to separate, the man promised to give his wife all that she needed—animals, utensils, provisions—but remained firm in his refusal to provide her with firewood, explaining that "this way her husband's absence will be more painful for her." Finally, the man controls all money earned by him through work on the hacienda or other business he conducts.

The woman is in charge of administering the family's agricultural products, being responsible for apportioning them in such a way as to provide for the whole year's subsistence. She can sell a small part of these products, taking them to the Sunday fair and bartering for products not made in the area, such as salt, kerosene, *ají*, kitchen utensils, and the like. Similarly, wool, cheese, eggs, and small animals such as chickens and guinea pigs are at her disposal, and she need not consult her husband before selling or using them. The cattle constitute something like a form of family savings, and all the women are interested in having their husbands buy them one or two cows to take care of, in order to make practical use of their spare time. The women also subtly pressure their husbands to acquire breeding bulls. The reason for this is that bulls provide a good guarantee of security for the family in case the husband dies; the widow will then be able to take advantage of the work that other men offer her by providing the services of the bulls in exchange. For this reason, many widowed women refer to their bulls as *qosay* (my husband).

Relations between spouses have a dual character. In public the husband behaves in a very authoritarian way toward his wife, never allowing her to interfere in his affairs by offering her opinion. The community supports such attitudes with sayings such as "the man is the one who talks" or "the woman should only bear children," which indicates that she should not participate in any extrafamilial relations. As a result of these attitudes, the woman is reticent, even in everyday situations, or else feigns total ignorance with regard to any situation whatsoever, including matters of the home which are her exclusive concern. The society as a whole tends to display an underestimation of the abilities of women, assigning them the less important tasks in the division of labor, which they perform humbly. The males boast of their authority and sometimes hit their wives while drunk.

However, within the privacy of the home the woman is

much more important than she would seem to be from her behavior in public. Her opinions are a decisive force in the behavior of the other members of the family, including the husband. She is consulted with regard to the management of the family economy, and her point of view must be taken into account concerning participation in the fiestas. It is true that the woman does not participate openly in public meetings, where she goes as an observer and remains apart from the group. However, after the men have reached an agreement, she can dissuade her husband from participating in activities which she does not favor. Many times we have observed that the men are hesitant to embark on a course of action, or even to reach a decision, because secretly they wish to consult with their wives in private first, after which they may change their attitudes radically. Thus, despite the protests and bravado of the men in public, the women actually have a great deal of influence over them, and control many situations with hidden threads.

2. Kuyo Chico children in line for milk distribution

The participation of the children in family activities begins early. From the age of five on, the boys take charge of watching and feeding the animals and carrying the water for domestic use. Usually the father begins to take them along to work with him when they are five or six years old, treating them as adults and friends to gain their confidence while instructing them in the technical skills they will need later on. Between ten and twelve years of age, the boys may begin to substitute for their father in work obligations he has contracted.

The girls learn how to spin and weave, as well as how to prepare food and take care of their younger brothers and sisters. Starting at eight to ten years old, they are almost exclusively responsible for the domestic chores, including cooking and care of the younger children. The parents tend to be indulgent with the misdeeds of the boys; whenever necessary, it is the father who disciplines the boys and the mother who disciplines the girls. Childhood games are viewed as a waste of time, and though they are not openly forbidden, the children are given useful activities and chores to keep them busy.

Cooperative Behavior

Much has been written about the *ayni* in Andean culture, as a reciprocal work relationship or a way of achieving economic cooperation. The ayni is this and much more. It is a subtle thread in the fabric of life, coloring the most basic human activities, from the lending and returning of work to the most delicate forms of reciprocity. It is said that "Life is an ayni," meaning that all activities are interwoven through this medium.

Reciprocity need not be a direct relation; it may include relations of courtesy or even repulsion. It is present when a person brings flowers to a wake, helps to dress the dead one, prays for him, and attends the funeral. It is that which brings people to attend a marriage and bring flowers for the newly-weds as an omen of fertility, or to contribute something of domestic use, such as a piece of wood or a bundle of straw, for the new home. A present has a meaning of reciprocity, of giving in order to receive, the understanding being always that when one gives something it is because he will require something in return. Similarly, affection is given in ayni, and one can acquire ill will through it. Ayni does not necessarily imply a prior agreement or design; one may enter into a relationship spontaneously, as one who gives with the certainty of receiving.

There are two modes of ayni, one concrete and one general. In the former, one knows precisely what one has given to whom and what one can expect to receive in return, as in the case of reciprocal work relationships, where work is offered which will be repaid with work of the same kind on a similar future occasion. The latter mode is more vague and impersonal—perhaps it is the society as a whole which contracts the obligation to reciprocate for what was done, perhaps it is even the spirits who control daily life and nature. The bad as well as the good which befalls a person has its form of retribution, though no one knows through whom it will arrive. Ayni is something pervasive and profound, built into the vary nature of things. Life itself is an ayni, and must be returned at death.

It is within the general context of this world view that we must understand the more specific concept of ayni as a relationship which one enters into by giving or doing something as an expression of solidarity, while having at the same time an expectation of future reciprocation. Another form of this relationship, the *mink'a,* is established when one solicits something. There are two general types of mink'a. The first involves the collaboration of various people for someone who solicits them and who then reciprocates their work with a fiesta at the end of the day, at which specially prepared foods, liquor, and chicha are served. The second is an interpersonal relationship involving the reciprocation of work. One individual may ask another to substitute for him in an obligation or to do some work for him, in exchange for which he will return the work in the same form at a future date.

The person who does this work or substitutes in his obligation is called his mink'a.

Other forms of collaboration include the *raymi* and the *wayka*. The *raymi* is a contribution of work toward a group festivity or celebration. This form of relationship has almost disappeared in the area, and has been replaced by the more concrete *hurk'a*. In this arrangement, a work contribution toward a celebration is solicited through the giving of a present, the acceptance of which seals the contract. The wayka is very common and involves the contribution of work on some project of general benefit to the group, such as the cleaning of a ditch or building of a road.

The Spanish term *faena* connotes external pressure or coercion. It is collective work (whether public or private) which the individual is obligated to do by way of intimidation, and carries no expectation of benefit. It is something imposed by the Mestizo authorities in their own interest. If the domination were to cease, the faena might come to have a more favorable image, as a way of getting individuals to contribute democratically to the general welfare of the community.

Living Conditions

The land, or Pachamama,[9] shelters all things and people, providing them with heat and making their lives easier; Thus the house comes to be identified with her. She guards and protects the people who dwell within it, sheltering them from the cold and warding off evil spirits while they sleep. They call her *cabildo* to show their veneration and respect. The house unites a family in all its pain and happiness, and is the only place where the married couple can copulate without provoking the anger of supernatural forces. After death, the person's spirit remains in the house for eight days until the ceremony of *P'acha-t'aqsay,* and returns each year thereafter on the Day of the Dead (Halloween) to partake of the food offered by the family.

9. The chief feminine deity of the Indian belief system. She is the protector of fecundity and of agricultural activities.

One cannot tamper with Pachamama's domain without first obtaining her consent and offering some tribute. Since all dwellings must rest on the earth, an offering is made to her during the construction of a new house, so that she will give strength to it. The tribute is placed in a pit dug near one corner of the house, and consists of a carefully prepared selection of coca leaves (*k'into*), vicuña fat, sweets, small breads, and certain tropical fruits. A ceremonial sprinkling (*t'inka*) of liquor and chicha on the ground is performed, invoking the deities (*Apus*) for protection. Then the construction of the house begins with the laying of the foundation, made of stone and mud set 50 cm. high. Atop this goes the first layer of adobe, which is followed by a second t'inka and invocation, the ceremony being repeated many times as the construction proceeds. When the walls are finished, they are often adorned with bouquets of flowers forming small crosses. Finally, when the roof is finished, a more elaborate and pompous t'inka is performed to celebrate the completion of the house. Friends and people who helped with the work are invited to the first fiesta in the new house, at which special foods are served, along with plenty of chicha and cane liquor to animate the festivities.

The houses are scattered throughout the community, and those clustered along the road tend to face in various directions. They are constructed of adobe with stone or mud foundations and thatched A-roofs. Seventy-five percent of the homes have only one room, while 20 percent have two, and only 5 percent have three. These rooms are small, averaging about nine by fifteen feet, and there are no windows. The doors are made of wood, and the doorways are built low and narrow (2 by 4.5 feet), so that one has to stoop in order to enter the dark interior.

There are generally two hearths located in the ground: one for the preparation of the day's meals and the other for making chicha. The walls are blackened by soot from these hearths, and smoke filters out through the thatched roof. Much-used bowls and utensils of clay or wood are scattered around the hearth, while others are stored in the niches which all of the homes have in their interior walls. One or two pestles for grinding grain sit on the floor, and earthen benches along the walls serve as seats. The guinea pigs which are always running around the floors of the homes live and sleep in a sheltered area beneath these benches.

Most of the people sleep on the floor, although some have bedsteads, raised adobe platforms or bed frames hung from stakes (*kawitos*). The beds generally consist of lamb skins or home-woven blankets. Clothing is hung on a stick or cord strung across the corner of the room, although some families who have no blankets sleep covered only by their daily clothes. Normally five or six people sleep in one room, which also serves as a kitchen, dining room, and reception area, and is also populated by small animals such as chickens and guinea pigs.

Each home has a small attic, or *marka*, which is constructed by suspending a woven floor from beams under the roof truss. This also forms a flat ceiling over the one-room interior, with a hole left in it for access to the attic. The marka has a special meaning in the home, because the seeds and the products of the harvest, as well as possessions which the family values, are stored there for safekeeping. Corn and seed left there are well-protected, since it is very dry, and the smoke which filters up from the hearths keeps insects away. Possessions are easily guarded, since the only entrance is through the house, and it is easy for the mother to control the use of the provisions stored in the marka. Thus the marka is tied directly to the security and survival of the family.

There are generally benches on the outside of the house, which serve as seats for fiestas, meetings, and other social gatherings. Thus, the outside of the house serves as a kind of reception area.

The general architectural pattern of the houses is the same: one-floor, rectangular construction with the roof running the long way and overhanging the walls to protect them from rain. The roofs are thatched with wheat or barley stems, although straw is used in a few cases, and allow water to drip through to the interior. One variation on this pattern is a house which is set into the slope of a hill and has only three walls. In this case water filters in over the floor.

The approximate cost of a one-room house is $56, including the wood, adobe, and thatching material. The lack of straw in the community raises the costs for those using this material, since it must be purchased at 25 or 29 cents a bundle from neighboring communities, as compared to 18 cents a bundle for wheat or barley stems. Approximately one hundred bundles are needed to construct a roof. Not included in these calculations is the value of the land on which the house sits, a value which is higher in Kuyo Chico because of the scarcity of land in the community. We had the opportunity to confirm this when a piece of land of forty square meters was sold for $168. The scarcity of land is another reason why most homes have only one room.

Regarding sanitary conditions, we found that 92 percent of the population deposited its excrement in the fields while 8 percent used animal pens near the houses. Marshes provide 05 percent of the drinking water, the river 15 percent. Bathing is done in the river by 79 percent of the population, in troughs or other household containers by 8 percent, and 13 percent does not bathe.

The Spiritual World

There are two aspects to the religious world of the Indians: one which we could call native, the other Christian.

The native religion integrates into a hierarchy a series of supernatural beings having limited jurisdictions and special areas of activity. Almost all of these spirits are incarnated in mountains and are identified generically as *Apus* or *Aukis,* according to their rank in the hierarchy. At the top is *Roal,* the Great Spirit Creator, incarnated in one of the highest mountains in the region, Ausangate, whose perpetual snows are visible over an extensive area. Roal is the universal creator who watches over all men and protects them constantly.

At the level immediately below Roal in the hierarchy are the Apus. The proper names of the Apus and Aukis are the same as the names of the mountains in which they reside. Apu-Qañaqway is charged with the care of the flocks, and is responsible for their fertility and procreation. Apu Qholqepunku watches over the health of humans, and Apu Wanakauri is responsible for their good-living. All three are found near Ausangate, and their jurisdiction is very extensive.

At the next lower level are the local Apus, who also have specialties but whose jurisdiction is more limited. In Kuyo Chico, the local Apus are Pukara-Pantillijlla, Koribian, and Apu Intiwatana, who are intimately related to the daily chores and anxieties of the men.

The attributes and powers of the Aukis also revolve around various areas of special jurisdiction, but the identity of these beings is unclear, as they tend to merge with the other deities and family ancestors.

Pachamama is on the same level as other Apus, but has a more general character. Being identified with the land, she is found everywhere, and her powers are related to agriculture. She herself is fertile, and is united in this way with the plants and female animals. She is a good being and loves people, on whom she lavishes sustenance. She enjoys gifts and likes to share with men the things which they drink. She does not have a concrete form, but perhaps is a woman who is always found sitting, to conserve the heat of her body, as she covers the seeds. Sometimes she presents herself in the form of a rock emerging from a farm plot. The people in Kuyo Chico remember that one time they tried to clear a plot on which there was a ñust'a (wiñaq-rumi, "stone that grows"), and the sky clouded over and torrential rains fell—but only in the vicinity of that plot. They desisted, since this must have been a ñust'a in which Pachamama was incarnated.

Alongside Pachamama is found Pacha-Tira, or simply Pacha. She is wicked and eats the hearts of men, who then die spitting blood. She is generally found by cliffs and precipices, and her preferred victims are children or adults who stay asleep in bad weather. There seems to be a close relation between these two beings, and when Pachamama is invoked along with the Apus by pouring portions of drink for her on the floor and sprinkling it with the fingers, the people are careful not to mention Pacha-Tira, which would be very dangerous. She is only mentioned when it is absolutely necessary, as when some tribute is offered to placate her, as during the building of a road or canal. On other occasions, she simply takes what she wants.

In addition to these chief deities, there are other supernatural beings who intervene in the lives of the people of Kuyo Chico and play an important role in their thinking and conduct. The *Soq'a* are beings who lived long ago. They have not died, but have dried out, and are physically identified with mummies. They may be of either sex, the males being called *Soq'a-machu* and the females *Soq'a-paya*. Eternally vigilant, their principal mission is to keep watch on the married. An act of infidelity brings the Soq'a to life again, in order that he may inflict punishment on the guilty one. If the adulterer is male, a Soq'a-paya takes the form of his wife or lover and incites him to copulation, after which she becomes pregnant. The man becomes ill, coughing and spitting blood. He begins to dry up little by little during the pregnancy, until at its conclusion the Soq'a-paya gives birth to a Soq'a-wawa and the man dies spitting foam and blood. If the adulterer is female, a Soq'a-machu presents himself to her in a similar manner. She suffers the same punishment as the man, but does not necessarily get pregnant. The prolonged absence of the husband may also stimulate the activity of a Soq'a-machu, who appears as the husband in the woman's dreams and impregnates her with a child who will be born malformed. Generally the child dies after birth, and the corpse is burned to prevent it from entering the world of the Soq'as, though, if it lives, it is incorporated into the world of men. The Soq'as cannot multiply among themselves because they have no blood.

Uma or *Qhepqe* are flying heads which detach themselves from the body to wander about while a person sleeps, gathering at the places where the *llipt'a*[10] are burned to discuss the

10. The ashes of specially selected shoots (usually quinua), used to prepare the muffins served as a condiment during the chewing of coca leaves.

destiny of the people and determine the dates and manner of their deaths. This may happen to anyone, but if the head should belong to an adulterous woman, it will become entangled by the hair among the thorns and brambles, and will be unable to return to its body. It is considered dangerous to walk around outside at midnight, especially for a woman, because *Qhepqe* might take over her body and convert her into a monster with two heads.

The world is populated by spirits and beings which contaminate the waters and environment. The dead walk at night and leave harmful emanations in their paths (*ohayqa*) which can cause death. The spirits of those who had an evil life can do harm to the animals, especially the breeding stock. Many things in nature can have supernatural powers; an old tree, a river, an ancient building, certain animals may possess such *animo*. Some rocks (*Wanka-rumi*) and topographical accidents such as gorges (*Apachita*) can grant favors, though it is necessary to make offerings to them. The spirit *Pujiu* inhabits the streams, and the people that he takes over become ill, with swelling in the stomach. The rainbow can kill people by causing the illness called *k'uychi,* and the winds can be harmful, especially those occurring at the changes of season, such as *Poqoywayra, Isu-wayra,* and *Soq'a-wayra,* which produce various aches, irritations, and skin diseases. Frosts, hail, and storms are unleashed by spirits to punish people for their bad living by harming the seeds. Many illnesses, such as smallpox, typhus, and typhoid fever, are personified, and only go away when they have been transferred to another person.

The *Enqaychus* or *Illas* are sacred figures, usually worked in stone, which play an important role in agriculture and cattle raising. They can have the form of an ear of corn, a potato, or some type of fruit, or of an animal for which fecundity is desired. If an abundant crop is desired, an Enqaychu of the appropriate form is placed in a hole at the edge of the plot. Enqaychu representations of animals for which fecundity is desired, especially cattle, are placed in spots where the animals usually pass, and come to life on foggy days to stimulate the animals. If a person enjoys the favor of Apu-Qañaqway, the Enqaychu may impregnate a female which will then give birth to a robust calf having some special distinction, such as a divided tail or notched ears. The offspring of the Enqaychu is usually male and is destined to serve exclusively as a breeder. In one case a man who owned one of these animals became rich by charging for the services of his bull. People from distant districts came in search of him, bringing their cows to be impregnated.

There are also natural Enqaychus, such as the *Intiwatana,* a rock which has the form of a bull. At *wañu* (fourth waning of the moon) and *pura* (full moon), he descends to the river to drink water, impregnating along the way the animals of people who are in good standing with the Apus. Man is related in diverse ways to all these beings which inhabit the world, and ties are established involving mutual obligations and expectations.

The world is populated with spirits that contaminate the natural environment. The dead walk in the night and leave in their tracks dangerous emanations which can cause death. Spirits of people who led evil lives cause harm to animals and even to their offspring. A large part of the natural world may have supernatural powers. Perhaps an old stricken tree, an old building, a river, certain animals, and so on possess *ánimo* (spirit). Certain boulders (*Wanka-Rumi*) or topographical features such as gorges may bring favor to man, but one must gain this favor through making an offering. Man is linked in various ways to the natural environment and even to the crops he himself planted. This linkage involves mutual obligations and expectations (*haychuy*).

The celebration of the native religion has a familial or quasi-familial character. It does not involve public participation, but is private, even clandestine. Nevertheless, we can affirm that the most profound religious convictions of the Indian involve this system of beliefs, which he has coupled very confusedly with Christianity, whose celebrations are public and involve collective participation. This is easy to understand if we take into account the fact that, during and after

the Spanish invasion, the Indian cults were zealously perse-
cuted, with Catholicism being imposed through fear and
violence by the "extirpators of idolatries," the doctrinaire
priests and the Holy Inquisition. Later, during the republic,
the Catholicism imposed by the invaders became the offcial
religion of the state, and, it should be noted, of the dominant
social groups. Even now it continues to be imposed, though
with different forms of coercion, bringing about the intermix-
ing of Christian doctrine with the prior religious beliefs of
the Indian. In the hierarchical ordering of the deities, and in
the tendency to assign specialized occupations to the saints,
we observe patterns similar to those in the Indian beliefs.
For example, St. Isidore is tied to agriculture, St. Mark to cattle raising, St. Cyprian to health, magic, and healing, and St.
Peter, the patron saint of the community, to the well-being of
the people. The Virgin Mary, frequently identified with Pachamama, at times with Pacha-Killa (the moon), is tied to feminine activities. However, though functions more or less
similar to those of the native deities are attributed to the Catholic saints, the saints do not have the same degree of importance as the Apus in each area.

The image of Christ is placed at the top of the Catholic
hierarchy; his jurisdiction is quite extensive and the powers
of the Creator are attributed to him. Many of his qualities are
confused with those of Roal, and it seems that the Indians
do not clearly distinguish between them. Thus it is the person-
ification of Christ which is most strongly connected to the
religiosity of the Indian. The devotion of the Indian finds its
deepest expression in the passages of the passion: Christ im-
prisoned, Christ whipped, Christ before the judges, Christ
crucified; expressed as Señor de Wanka, Señor de la Senten-
cia, Señor de Unupunku, and Señor de Qoyllurit'i. Related
to these images is a sense of the abundance of justice, which
can be explained historically. The Inca society had developed
a high degree of justice and equality which was shattered
with the arrival of the Spaniards, who brought abuse, op-
probrium, brutality, exploitation, and injustice. But they also
brought a Christ who, loving justice, suffered the injustice of

men, as is depicted with pathos in the stories, paintings, and images of the passion. It is possible that the Indian, tormented by the conquerors, incorporated Christ into his religion with a certain ease, assigning to him the function of God of Justice.

Christ and the Catholic saints are the only deities who receive public festivals of celebration, and these are arranged through a system of religious *cargos*. A cargo (duty) is the responsibility which one person assumes to host the fiesta. He may obtain the help of other members of the community by means of the hurk'a—an agreed obligation to contribute to the fiesta, that is, to pay for the candles, provide a group of dancers or part of the wardrobe for the icon, arrange the platform of the saint, and so on.

The fiesta of St. Peter in June is the celebration of the patron saint of Kuyo Chico. The cargo is transferred annually from some persons to others, and no one can refuse to assume it. Someone who will not accept the cargo is strongly censured by the group, suffering what might be called a social death as a result of these pressures vigorously stimulated by the parish priest. Individuals usually accept the cargo against their will, and sometimes someone proposes the name of a person out of a desire for revenge or some other shameful feeling. The designation for a cargo almost always means the ruin of the man and his family, since they must suffer many privations and hardships to fulfill their obligations.

The preparations begin immediately upon receipt of the cargo, as one must accumulate considerable amounts of firewood, stock enough purple corn to make the chicha, consign various sheep and two or three cows to the slaughter, and save up the money necessary to provide the food and drink to be consumed during the celebration (liquor, chickens, guinea pigs, potatos, beans). In addition there are the costs of the mass, the buying of the candles, a donation for the wardrobe of the icon, payments to the sacristans and musicians, and the parish priest's fee, which is raised for the occasion. Finally, not only must the entire town be fed and made drunk for several days, but sometimes meat must be distributed for the families to take to their homes.

The mechanism of the taking of cargos is not limited to the religious life of the town, but extends to the regional celebrations as well, which are the occasions for large pilgrimages by the Indians of Kuyo Chico. The fact that there will be many people from the community at the celebrations of Wanka in San Salvador and Qoyllurit'i in Okongate makes the designated one unable to refuse his cargo. Though he must bear only part of the responsibility for these regional celebrations, the expense involved is great.

It would not be exaggerating to say that the great religious festivals offer not only a chance for social recreation, but the opportunity to earn the respect and esteem of the community—respect and esteem which could put the Indian in a position analogous to that of the ruined nobleman.

The district priest officiates at all celebrations, aided by one or two sacristans and often the *económo,* who is the administrator of the church treasury and receives some of the parish lands to exploit for his own benefit. It is through these functionaries that the Indian establishes relationships with the world of saints and Catholic images, at masses, baptisms, marriages, and funerals.

Relations with the supernatural deities of the native religion are established through a hierarchy of specialists known as *Yachaq* or *Paqo,* and are more involved with daily activities. At the top position is the *Altomisayoq,* who has the power to conjure the great spirits of the mountains, the Apus, including Roal, the Creator Spirit. He calls them together to consult about important events or to establish the diagnosis, cause, and treatment of serious illnesses. The *Pampamisayoq* occupies a lower position and has the power to call lesser deities, such as the local Apus and the Aukis. His activities also involve less important events. The *Wishch'oq* is a specialist in divination, consulted to help locate lost animals or identify robbers.

Unlike the three *Yachaq* we have just mentioned, the *Layqa* or sorcerer (*hechicero*) is a malevolent being, related to Pacha and the devil (*supay*) and capable of causing illness or death by his witchcraft. He can diagnose diseases and prescribe cures by means of the magic *Qollpa,* a compound of sulphur and iron or potassium which is boiled with the patient's urine, allowing the Layqa to "see" the answers in the froth. He grants people certain powers by means of the amulets he gives, and those who resort to his sorcery can obtain love, money, or dominion over others. The people hate and fear the *Layqa,* while they have much respect and admiration for the Altomisayoq, Pampamisayaq and Wishch'oq. It is interesting to note that the prestige of a Yachaq is almost always lowest in his own community, where he is generally ignored. The Yachaq who are considered "good" always live in distant districts, while people come from far off to Kuyo Chico to solicit the services of the local specialists.

Although this is not the proper place, we should mention another type of specialist, the *Hampeq* or *curandero* (medicine man or healer), who enjoys great prestige in the community. He performs many types of cures using special herbs, soils, fruits, and medicines from the jungle and sea, and practices surrounded by magic and superstition. He generally learns his craft from a teacher, and can bequeath it by teaching it to his children or disciples. The Yachaq, on the other hand, receives his powers from supernatural forces.

Education

The school of Kuyo Grande, over thirty years old, and a newer one in Amphay, are sectional schools subordinate to the Central Peasant School of Pisaq (*Núcleo Escolar Campesino*), which functions in the district capital. For twelve years a coeducational school had been functioning in Kuyo Chico, directly subordinate to the Office of Education for the province (*Inspección Provincial de Educación*).

According to the registers, fifty students were matriculated in 1959, with an average daily attendance of seventeen. Three students completed sufficient study to take exams. The school served the neighboring communities of Qotobamba and Mask'a in addition to Kuyo Chico.

The school building was a small enclosure, 11-by-25-foot,

3. Pre-project school

with a dirt floor and no lighting. It had been the home of one of the Indians, who had granted it to be used as a school. The children sat on adobe benches and wrote on *qharapas*, desks made of strips of bark which are the waste material from tree cutting. Four second-year students were privileged to use ramshackle desks.

As a primary school, it handled the first three years of study: "transition" (similar to kindergarten), first, and second grades. Classes were conducted by a Mestizo schoolteacher, who dictated to the students assembled in the one room without even the most basic teaching materials, except for a 16-by-20-inch blackboard which had been lent by one of the Indians, who had acquired it earlier thinking that it might be of use to his children some day.

When the school was started, the teacher in charge was able to arouse the interest of the Indians in helping to obtain a suitable site for a new school. Given the scarcity of land, it was necessary to make a series of transactions and exchanges

44

before acquiring the barely sufficient area upon which the building was erected. It took eight years to construct and roof three rooms, one destined to be the administrative office of the school. During this period, the teacher solicited the aid and technical assistance of SECPANE (*Servicio Cooperativo Peruano-Norteamericano de Educación*). This group helped to draw the plans for the building and contributed $56 toward the purchase of roof tiles.

When the construction of the school began, there was a great deal of enthusiasm on the part of the Indians, but when the children learned very little, interest dwindled, until finally there was practically no desire to send the children to school. The teacher appealed to the lieutenant governor of Pisaq and the *cabecillas* of Kuyo Chico, Qotobamba, and Mask'a for help, asking them to confiscate household objects and hold them until the *peasant* children were matriculated. Similar methods were used to deal with the problem of poor attendance, but even so, regular attendance was never obtained. The parents constantly claimed that the children didn't learn anything at school and only went there to waste time, and that they were needed at home to do domestic chores and attend to the *chacras* (small farm plots). There was greater resistance to the girls having to go to school, because their parents felt that learning to read and write would be of no use to them, since in the daily activities of the family it is the males who deal with problems and handle relations with outsiders.

The few people in these communities who knew how to read and write had gone to school in Pisaq, or learned while in the army or working in the cities. Despite the length of time that the school had been functioning in Kuyo Chico, 94 percent of the populations of Kuyo Chico, Qotobamba, and Mask'a were illiterate Quechua speakers.

The fact that the Indians had worked on the construction of a new school but eventually lost interest when it went unfinished seemed promising to us. If a new school had once seemed important to the community, perhaps our program could arouse interest again.

3

The Program of Applied Anthropology

The Web of the Power Structure

In the first part of this book, we indicated how the existing distribution of power in the area amounted to total domination by the Mestizo class. The Indians, saddled with work duties and obligations to the town authorities and Mestizos, had very little time left over to attend to their own labors, and almost none to work for the general benefit of their community. Faced with this situation, it was impossible for us to consider initiating a program of change without first confronting this problem squarely. The condition of the Indian in this region resulted not only from his occupying the lowest social level, but also to a large extent from the attitudes of the Mestizos, who considered him inferior and without rights. The Mestizo had to be made to understand that the Indian has basic human rights and not just obligations, and that the Mestizo should put an end to the exploitation for which he was responsible.

Often we hear rhetorical declarations about equality before the law. In the case of the Indian, such declarations are far removed from reality, for those people charged with enforcing the law have not freed themselves of the Mestizo prejudices against the Indian. Thus while we agree with the aim of helping the Indian to achieve his liberation, we insist that at the same time efforts must be made to make the Mestizo respect the law. Economic inferiority, ignorance of his rights, and strong social pressures do not allow the Indian recourse to the abundant legislation which protects him, and he is easy prey for those Mestizos without scruples who have learned how to work with the authorities for their mutual benefit. Given the excesses and miscarriages of justice which were constantly committed in our community, we had to assume a vigorous attitude of requiring the authorities and Mestizos to enforce and obey the law. The task required a sustained effort which was difficult and vexing, but we felt that although such action was extremely time-consuming, it might help to arouse interest in our program in the Indian communities and to show that there were some Mestizos who had favorable attitudes toward the Indian. We knew that the Indians would not be able to improve their situation alone, that someone was needed to deal with contingencies as they arose—someone with a knowledge of the laws who could see to it that they were enforced and the rights of the Indians recognized, until the Indians themselves were capable of exercising this power. Thus it became necessary to meet power with power. Despite the hopes we had had when we arrived, that as anthropologists all we would have to do was enter into friendly relations with all involved, reality made us understand that this was not possible.

Our decision recognized the need to alter the existing situation, for the participation of the Indian himself was required if we were to introduce changes, and this in turn required time beyond that which he already spent working for the Mestizos or providing for his family, time to be spent learning to read or attending community assemblies. The assemblies were absolutely vital to our program, for they presented opportunities to interchange ideas and to raise new possibilities.

We had decided to oppose power with power, but had no power at our disposal, and so had to create the appearance of power. To do this, we made use of the fact that the program was sponsored by the Peruvian Indian Institute under the Ministry of Labor and the University of Cuzco, according

to the National Plan for Integration as it had been constituted
shortly before the start of the program. This national plan
had been sponsored by several state institutions, including
the Ministry of War, the Ministry of Public Education, the
Ministry of Agriculture, the Ministry of Labor and Indian
Affairs, and the Institute of Agrarian Reform, as well as the
Agrarian Development Bank. The fact that the Institute came
under the plan, and that by presidential directive the Ministry
of Labor and Indian Affairs was charged with coordinating
all of the actions involved, enabled us to invoke the image of
the combined power of all of these institutions. To accom-
plish this, we presented the local authorities with a tran-
script of the directive through which the National Plan for
Integration was created, which included mention of the Kuyo
Chico program.[1] Because this was a good opportunity to make
the Mestizo authorities understand that our program had a
lot of power behind it, I also sent each authority a circular,
asking his collaboration to avoid abuses committed against
the Indians, such as forced labor. I enclosed the text of law
no. 1183 which prescribes imprisonment and withdrawal of
eligibility for public office for those authorities guilty of recruiting or providing Indians for public or private works.[2]
The circulars having been sent, we could undertake more
direct actions on the district, provincial, and departmental
levels. We also had the opportunity at this time to require the
enforcement of a law regarding other rights frequently violated, particularly patrimonial and property rights, which are
essential to the Indian economy since they insure a margin
of security to the individual and his family. Such security
was a prerequisite for the introduction of the program of
change we had planned.

Having proceeded in the way described, I next managed
to have an assembly called in Kuyo Chico, which was packed
with Indians from the neighboring communities. When the

1. See the Appendix.
2. See Manual D. Velasco Nuñez, *Compilación de la Legislación Indigenista Concordada*, (Lima: Peru), p. 2.

people had gathered and the assembly was about to begin, the mayor of Pisaq, the district justice of the peace, the town governor, and the chief of police arrived. Undoubtedly these authorities had come to control the proceedings, or at least to inhibit free discussion, but I took advantage of the situation by proceeding to tell the Indians that no one had the right to force them to work without pay, or to take things from their homes, or to mistreat them, or to imprison and require personal work of them, and that the authorities present were obliged to see to it that their rights were not violated, since these abuses were forbidden by law. Then I enumerated all of the illegal actions and abuses which had been committed in the area, indicating that the authorities were obligated to enforce the law and obey it themselves if they didn't want to end up in jail.

The manner in which I discussed the subject in front of the authorities gave, in my judgment, a greater credibility to my words, a sense of reality which they would not have had if the authorities had not been present. I proceeded to take further advantage of the situation by asking the authorities to affirm my words or speak out if what I had said was untrue. Of course they had no alternative but to affirm publicly what I had said.

From then on it was necessary to use all the resources at our disposal to counter the pressure exerted on the Indians. We made charges before the criminal courts, presented cases to the ministerial authorities, and, in some cases, went so far as to use physical force. On one such occasion I was on my way into the town of Pisaq with the agricultural engineer when we saw a crowd of Indians gathered at the entrance to the town and stopped to see what was happening. We were told that the lieutenant governor was seizing their products and paying them extremely low prices for them. The lieutenant governor was there, and when we asked him what he was doing, he replied, "These Indians are monopolizers and speculators," whereupon he produced a Lima newspaper in which there appeared an article describing measures being

4. Núñez del Prado speaking to community assembly

used to crack down on the monopolies and speculation which
were raising the cost of living. He was using this argument
to rob the Indians of their goods, which he was placing in
a house by the side of the road. We told him that what he was
doing was illegal, because these Indians were neither monopolizers nor speculators, but were carrying their products on
their backs to the market in Pisaq. I said that he should return the articles he had taken and made an attempt to enter
the house, whereupon he placed himself in the doorway to
impede me. I found myself obliged to hit him, and he fell down
inside the house. At this point the governor arrived, and,
hearing of the incident, came toward me. However, it was his
bad luck that the engineer was standing nearby and moved
in quickly to halt him. I immediately ordered the Indians who
were present to take their things back and leave. They did so
and in a few minutes were gone.

The next day I received a summons to appear before the prefect[3] of Cuzco for resisting the authorities. I was also charged with trespassing, for having ordered the Indians to go into the house to retrieve their possessions. After being rebuked by the prefect, I replied that what I had done was to impede an individual who was committing a crime, namely, assaulting the Indians. I asserted that although this individual was the lieutenant governor, he had abused his authority by committing this crime and thus, at the point of my intervention, this authority had been nullified.

Before leaving Kuyo Chico, I had formulated a plan to take advantage of this occasion to produce a break in the chain of authority from the prefect to the governor. For this purpose I brought along a photostatic copy of a document which had come into our possession some months earlier, concerning the enganchadores working in the Pisaq area for the prefect's own hacienda.[4] During the course of our conversation, I made it clear that the governor and lieutenant governor were putting the prefect's reputation in jeopardy, to the point that they could get him into serious trouble concerning their enganchador activities. I handed him the photostat, and he became visibly startled upon reading it. It seemed that the prefect owned an hacienda in the jungle region of Q'osñopata, and that the governor was the person in charge of the enganchador activities in Pisaq. It was a communication to this effect, written by the governor himself, that had fallen into our hands. I suggested that the prefect dismiss these authorities, and permitted myself to propose as a replacement for the governor a man over whom we had some influence. About a week later, the governor and lieutenant governor were removed from their posts.

We also had to deal with a series of abuses by people who were strangers to the locality. For example, in the neighboring community of Amphay, a teacher had set himself up as

3. The chief executive of the department, analogous to governor of a U.S. state.
4. See the Appendix, document 4.

a sort of chief, taking over the lands and administering justice himself. He required tribute and labor of the Indians, and established a fine equivalent to twenty-five cents (U.S.) per day for a child's absence from school. He also required these *peasants* to work on his own lands.

On one occasion, a child stayed home from school for three days because he was ill. The mother did not have enough money to pay the fine, so she sent the child back to school with a hen. As punishment for not having brought the money, the teacher stripped the child and whipped him until he bled, sending him home naked and badly hurt. The mother decided not to send him to school again.

Some time later, the teacher showed up at the house to inquire about the child. The mother informed him that she had decided not to send him to school anymore. The teacher offered to take the child back, promising not to punish him anymore. Before leaving, he proposed that she sell him a pig which he happened to notice. Wanting to get in his favor, the woman turned over the animal, indicating that she would charge 80 soles ($3) for it. The teacher accepted the price, took the pig, and left. Several days later the women went to him to collect her money, whereupon he refused to pay, claiming that it was his birthday, that the community was obligated to celebrate it with some tribute, and that the pig in question would serve the purpose perfectly.

This was one of many incidents cited in an eighteen-page complaint against this teacher which we registered with the Office of Basic and Adult Education (*Dirección de Educación Fundamental y del Adulto*), requesting a replacement. As a result the teacher was transferred to a distant community and we heard no more of him.

Abuse and injustice occurred at all social levels and in many forms. Differences between Indians could be settled by conciliation or could be taken before the Office of Indian Affairs, but conflicts arising from pressures exerted by Mestizos required the legal aid and protection of our program to counterbalance the existing distribution of power and influence. The manner in which we operated gained us the sympathy of the Indians and antagonized the Mestizos, who were personally affected by changes in ways which they considered contrary to their own interests.

"Paternalism" has frequently been discussed and condemned in the literature of Indian studies, but we feel that this point needs more careful consideration. Tutelage and the exercise of protection are the necessary results of the limitations which the Indian suffers because of his situation. The position of the illiterate peasant is somewhat analogous to that of a minor, who is limited by both his legal status and his lack of certain knowledge and skills. Indians are ignorant of many of their rights, as well as of how to exercise them.

We must remember that power is held by the Mestizos, who are charged with carrying out the laws and court decisions, and that they will prefer to ignore or oppose these laws if it is in their own interest to do so. A specific example can demonstrate the validity of this statement. Directives concerning the salaries and minimum wage for the Indians have been on the books for nearly forty years. The first article of law no. 2285 says that "the personal work of the Indians shall be remunerated in cash, and it is absolutely prohibited to require them to live in agricultural, industrial, or ranching centers against their will." The first article of a presidential directive of May 11, 1923, establishes that "the municipal councils of the Andean provinces shall issue annually at their opening January sessions ordinances fixing the minimum daily wage for Indian laborers in the areas of agriculture, transportation, and herding. This wage shall be the average of what is paid in all parts of the province." Despite these clear directives, not one municipal council in the entire history of Peru has deliberated on the minimum wage for the Indian. The reason is obvious: to establish a minimum wage would mean to have to pay it. Since it is the very same Mestizos who exploit the Indians and serve on the municipal councils, these laws have simply become dead letters.

The interests of the dominant groups constitute a permanent barrier to change, helping to maintain the present status of the Indians, whose economic inferiority, together with ignorance of rights and strong social pressures, do not allow them equal access to the law. Because all of this works against the autonomy of the Indian, we believe that an initial period of protection and aid, or "paternalism" if you wish, is necessary, until little by little the Indian learns to walk alone.

First Project: Home Improvement

The principal means of livelihood in Kuyo Chico is agriculture, and it would have been reasonable for us to initiate our work in this area, which is one of great concern and interest to the people. However, because of the extreme scarcity of land in the community, we decided that this was not the best way to proceed. Property had been broken down into small parcels, and we were informed that the Indians had made a series of exchanges in order to obtain a small site for the new school, barely sufficient to erect three rooms. This made it clear to us that we would not be able to make use of large plots to demonstrate the advantages of certain agricultural techniques and crops. Magnificent explanations and ideas can be conveyed in formal discussions, but these verbal matters would not have had the impact in promoting our program that actual agricultural demonstrations could achieve.

We wanted to initiate our program in an area that would carry over into other realms and serve as the stimulus for additional projects. During our earlier studies of the community, we had discovered the important fact that ceremonial emphasis is placed upon the construction of the home. Since ceremony indicates a profound interest shared by the group, we decided to plan an initial project of this kind.

Eventually we formulated the following work plan. We would enter into agreements with the villagers to the effect that they would turn over their houses to us for renovation. We would assume responsibility for part of the work and delegate the rest to the owner of the house. Among the responsibilities to be left to the owner were the making of the roof, the doors, the windows, the floors, the stucco, the flat ceilings, and the openings in the walls for doors and windows, as well

5. Men of Kuyo Chico preparing building materials

as the painting. We would pay for the renovation and provide a mason to work along with the owner, allowing him an opportunity to learn special techniques of masonry. In return for our investment, we would occupy the house during the period of renovation. Thus the money which we invested would be considered rent for the house, and it could not be thought that we were giving something away. From the owner's point of view, the house itself would pay for the renovation.

The object of this program was not to renovate the houses, although this would be a good side effect. We considered the improvement of the homes a means to various ends, among them the organization of a communal effort and the creation of a chain of incentives which would set the stage for further projects. We intended to demonstrate the usefulness of establishing a focal point of social interest, by which we mean an area of activity which offers the possibility of combining a series of linked stimuli to guide the community toward innovations adapted to their own culture.

We proposed our plan at the first assembly, and the idea was greeted with much enthusiasm. Everyone seemed interested in entering into the proposed arrangement to remodel their homes. But when the time came to turn over their houses to us, no one stepped forward. A month and a half went by, during which we continued to explain our proposal to the people, carefully stimulating interest in the possibilities presented. We showed a Walt Disney film about tuberculosis which explained the way in which the disease is spread. The film clearly demonstrates the advantages of a well-illuminated and ventilated house, by showing in drawings the way in which the rays of the sun kill the tuberculosis germs, and how these germs can spread through poorly lighted and unclean houses. It also shows how the germs invade the respiratory system and take over and destroy the lungs, which explains why the victim coughs and spits blood and eventually dies. We had seen the movie before and made the necessary explanations to the Indians in Quechua. We repeated the showing three or four times, and it had a big impact on the viewers.

Thereafter we continued to talk informally with the Indians, without emphasizing our plan too strongly. Then, at another assembly, we again made our proposal, and this time there was one person who decided to accept it. He was none other than Tomás Díaz, the cabecilla of the community, who had also been the first person whom we had contacted upon our arrival in Kuyo Chico.

Here we must say something about Don Tomás and his position in the community, so that the significance of his participation is fully understood. Earlier we explained that the cabecilla is basically nothing more than an instrument of the authorities in the district capital. Tomás found his job very distasteful. He spoke to us about his painful situation, and told us how difficult it was for him to have to confiscate objects from his brothers or take them prisoners to be sent to the faenas in the town. He was often given the most detestable tasks. He had to collect chickens, guinea pigs, and lambs as tribute for the authorities, who paid little or nothing in return. He had to exert pressure on the people to make them comply with the caprices of the Mestizos. In short, he had to carry out whatever tasks were assigned to him, no matter how distasteful.

The people understood his situation all too well, and thus did not hate him. They knew that he was only an instrument, and that he performed his job because he was powerless to resist the authorities. Don Tomás knew all of the people in the community, and had cordial relations with them on a personal level, many being close relatives of his. He came from the most respected family in the community, and much of the esteem which he enjoyed was a result of his ties with the Qhapa family on his mother's side. However, Tomás Díaz Qhapa enjoyed the respect of the community not only for his friendships and family ties, but also for the way in which he conducted himself as *cabecilla,* having valiantly defended the community against violent plunder by a neighboring hacendado. He had shown extraordinary diligence and willingness to sacrifice for the community in the judicial confrontation with the hacendado, going so far as to sell the few cattle he owned to pay the court costs, which the community could not or would not cover, believing the case to be a lost cause from the start.

We began work on the house, taking care to preserve certain traditional patterns and architectural elements which were of aesthetic or practical importance, such as the wall niches inside the house or certain preferred colors. We wanted the completed house to look pretty not by our tastes but by those of the community. For example, we took care to select colors which were popular among the people, finding that the most preferred colors were brilliant blue and fire orange, or *chiwanway,* which is mentioned as a special color in many songs and folk tales. Tomás himself worked with us on the house, which began to look nicer and nicer to the community. Shortly thereafter, many other people decided to accept our proposal.

We left the roofing and the making of doors and windows to the individual owners. In this region of the mountains, the rains are very heavy during the wet season. With the first wet season after the remodeling, the rains swept away the paint and stucco and flat ceilings, converting all that had been so pretty into a complete disaster. This was because of the wheat and barley thatching used to construct the roofs, which is not waterproof. Furthermore, the financial loss involved was considerable, the total cost of one roof being about $19, at 19 cents per bundle of thatch.

Linked Projects

Kuyo Chico was one of the poorest communities in the region, and so we had to attack problems multilaterally to have any hope of initiating an effective and orderly process of development. Only by dealing with many problems simultaneously can we bring about improvements without the crisis and dislocation that result from one-sided development. With this aim in mind, we examined the economic situation in the region. We had noted that there is an ordinance in the city of

Cuzco which states that all houses must be roofed with tile. This offered us the possibility of an open market able to absorb a constant production of tiles. After arranging to remodel homes in the way we have described, we decided to encourage the community to develop a small tile industry in order to achieve some economic security. It was for this reason that we deliberately left the roofing up to the owners of the homes. The destructive action of the rains worked to our advantage because it made people think seriously about the advisability of changing their roofing materials. We seized the opportunity to suggest that they make their own tiles, since this would save money and actually cost less than thatching. A house could easily be roofed using no more than a thousand tiles at an approximate cost of $17. We had investigated and found that we would be able to contract a tile-making specialist from San Sebastián (another district in Cuzco) to direct the construction of a furnace and teach the community how to make tiles. When we suggested this at the assembly, the community accepted our proposal.

The instructor came to the community and directed the construction of the first oven and the making of the first batch of tiles. A special place was prepared for the drying of the tiles. The people worked collectively on these projects, under the system of wayka.[5] Six thousand tiles were ready to be processed when it was discovered that it was impossible to gather enough fuel to keep the fire going for the time required to bake the tiles. Thus it was necessary to buy the fuel from another area, and the *peasants* had to make some economic sacrifices in order to do this. Finally they bought the necessary fuel from an hacienda eight kilometers away, having to carry it back to Kuyo Chico themselves.

In this way the community was brought to face clearly the lack of combustible material in Kuyo Chico, and began to consider the necessity of finding some way to provide for their future needs. They decided that the best course of action

5. See "Cooperative Behavior" in chapter 2 above.

was to make a large planting of eucalyptus trees. To carry out this project, we made an agreement with SCIPA (*Servicio Cooperativo Interamericano de Producción de Alimentos*), which brought us eight thousand eucalyptus and two thousand pines, to be planted on a slope at the head of the community, graded down towards the river. There was good reason to think that the *peasants* would take care of the plants, for they believe that once a seed is planted, a relationship is established between it and the man who planted it, who must do everything in his power to see that it grows. A failure to do so would result in *haychuy*, that is, the plant would resent this treatment and communicate these feelings to the other plants which the man has cultivated.

They solved the problem of irrigation by carrying water from the river in pitchers, cans, and any other containers they could find. This difficult and fatiguing work revived interest in an old project surrounded by fears: the building of an irrigation canal. It seems that once before they had begun the digging of a canal, but had forgotten to pay proper tribute to Pacha-tira, who showed her wrath by exacting her own tribute: one man was killed in an accident while working on the canal. Wanting to take advantage of this renewed interest in the canal, we hired a local specialist, Juancho Halanoqa, to offer the necessary tribute, in order to lessen the fears of the people and give them a sense of security with respect to the work. The ceremonial offering was made in 1960, by burying a guinea pig at the beginning of the canal to placate the fury of Pacha.

Plans having been made, the community began the work on the canal, which was to be almost five kilometers long. Because it was to be dug in a very rocky zone, drilling experts were contracted by the program to aid in the project by using explosives to break the rock. The engineer assumed direction of the work, which was later taken over by a member of the program, Leonardo Choquetinco, the general superintendent. In 1963, a Peace Corps volunteer, Michael Mantesch, assisted the superintendent, obtaining a motorized drill which greatly speeded up the work Even so, because the community could not devote full time to the project, it was estimated that the canal would not be completed and inaugurated until November 1965.

We should note here that the purpose of the canal was not to irrigate the groves that had been planted, but to make available close to thirty hectares of land (seventy-four acres) which had been uncultivable for lack of water (which was the case with most of the community's lands). In addition, this irrigation would guarantee the harvests of the lands which had already been cultivated.

The canal had not yet been finished, but already the community was thinking of new possibilities, such as establishing a hydroelectric plant and using the energy to operate a flour mill. Though there was neither power plant nor mill, they proceeded to erect a building for a bread bakery.

The tile factory produced very favorable results. It was established as a community-owned business, with individuals taking turns working at it under the general administration of the cabecilla. The tiles were sold in Cuzco for $33.50 per thousand, and to community members for $22.40 per thousand. Revenues were deposited under the control of the cabecilla, to build up a contingency fund to meet any expenses that the community might incur during the year and a half that the company was in their hands. At that point, by general accord at the assembly, the factory was made into an open business, that is, the community members became potential businessmen who could ask to use it, leaving 7 percent of the gross sales income, according to the system of ayni. After some time, the community modified this system, forming small groups of six to eight people who would take over the factory. They were to pay the indicated 7 percent of sales income to the community and work as employees of their business, at assigned wages to be paid upon sale of the tiles. Profits were to be left for distribution in an annual liquidation. After a year of functioning in this manner, we calculated the profits of two of these groups at $76 and $114. We had expected each group member to claim his share, but to our surprise discovered that they were saving the money to form a fund, with the ultimate aim of purchasing church-owned lands.

Perhaps the most important result of the successful manufacture of tiles is the sense of economic security which the people of Kuyo Chico now have. The existence of this source of revenue in their own community has reduced both the surplus labor force and the need for land on the neighboring haciendas. We have already explained how the relations between the landowners and the *peasants* require of the latter between 90 and 120 days of labor per year per topo of land used. These requirements have become less strict and salaries have risen as the need for labor has increased, due to the fact that the Indian is no longer forced to work without pay. Where an Indian was paid 1.8 U.S. cents, the salaries now offered range from 45 to 56 cents. As a result of these changes, the average annual income per capita today is approximately five times what it was in 1959.

The home remodeling project also created interest in other areas because our agreement had left the responsibility for making the doors and windows to the owners. This presented problems for the Indians, who did not have the technical knowledge and material resources necessary to make wooden doors and windows. They tried going to the carpenters in Pisaq, but found they could not pay the high costs of labor. This difficulty was brought up in one of the assemblies, and someone suggested that if they had the necessary tools and someone to direct the work, the owners of the houses could make the doors and windows themselves, using their own wood. We replied by offering the possibility of establishing a carpentry workshop in the community, run by an instructor who could assist and direct the peasants in whatever projects they wanted to undertake. It seemed best to set up a small rustic workship equipped with simple tools, so that later on the peasants could acquire their own tools and be able to operate with the technical skills and material resources available to them. We knew that once the remodeling was finished and they had adapted to the somewhat new living conditions, they would see a need for further changes. Already the perceived needs of the community were changing, as there were some who wanted to make tables, chairs, shelves, beds, and other furniture and utensils for their homes. Anyone wanting to make something had only to bring his wood to the workshop and ask the journeyman carpenter for assistance. This arrangement did not rule out the possibility of some of the young men learning carpentry in a more formal way, and some did apprentice themselves and eventually take up carpentry as a trade. The workshop was also used once a week by the school, with the program providing the children with the wood necessary to make small objects.

Although the aim of the first project was the initiation of further projects and not home improvement, the achievements in this area were significant. Of the sixty-two houses existing in the community when we arrived, thirty were improved. Although this represents not quite 50 percent over a period of ten years, there are some factors which should be considered in the evaluation of these results. First of all, a person who decided to improve his house had to move out and rent it to us during the period of remodeling, generally going to live with relatives or in some provisional shelter he had raised. Second, the time required to remodel a house varied according to the amount of time which the owner could devote to the work—generally only a few days per month.

Nevertheless, the remodeling created enough interest so that some people decided to build new houses, following architectural patterns which departed from tradition. For example, we have noted that there is now a tendency to build homes with several rooms, each assigned to a different purpose. The new houses are designed with illumination and ventilation in mind, with large doors and glass windows of various sizes. Many have two floors, although the ceiling tends to be much lower on the second floor than on the first. This may be because the second floor is supported by the roof beams, which extend to form the eaves of the house. If the house is built too high, the eaves will be too short to protect the walls. It is also likely that the people still equate the second floor with the traditional *marka.*

This significant interest in home improvement has diminished markedly more recently, because the people in the community expect to build a new and more modern town on lands acquired from the church in 1968. Thus they are waiting for the final plans to be drawn up and new parcels of land allotted to them.

The idea of building a new town is particularly attractive because present water and electric-light services cannot be distributed to all of the homes in the community, since they are so scattered. A spring currently serves as the single source of clean water for the community, and efforts are being made to locate additional sources. A reservoir is planned to control the supply of water, but this project cannot be carried out without a new, more centralized town. There is a desire to have potable water close at hand, a desire aroused by the benefits obtained from the construction of the first and only water spigot in the locality. Similarly, there is a desire to have electricity in each of the new homes, a service which is available only to the homes located close together in the present community. The people living in scattered houses continue to use traditional forms of illumination. Thus the new town is planned to have the houses close together, in order to allow good streets and light, water, and sewage services.

We should clarify here the situation with regard to electric lighting. It had seemed important to us that the *peasants* become interested in the benefits of electricity, for at the same time this would encourage new attitudes with regard to the mechanisms of exchange in modern life. We acquired a gasoline-motor generator, and electricity was installed in the homes and offices of the field personnel. Electric light was also installed along the central sector of the road, and this restricted service was maintained for a short period of time. Then we proposed in an assembly that members of the community who wanted electric light could obtain cords and bulbs and ask to be connected to the power line. Almost all of the peasants in the lower part of the community accepted the free electricity during the next three years. Then, in an assembly, we explained that this service had become a burden on the program which could be alleviated if those people who benefit from the service would contribute a monthly payment of 7.5 U.S. cents per 50-watt bulb. There was some disagreement about this, so we said that those who did not want to pay for the service could notify us, and their electricity would be disconnected. Close to 50 percent of the *peasants* who had been using electric light asked for suspension of the service. However, after fifteen days of going back to candles and kerosene, the same people started coming in to request a renewal of the service and announce their willingness to pay the required fee. This case shows quite clearly how it is necessary in some circumstances to offer free services in a very paternalistic way, with the aim of using the needs created to stimulate progress toward new forms of life.

The Literacy Campaign, Education and Civic Participation

The manner in which we have been discussing our program suggests that the linked projects were carried out successively, whereas in actuality these actions were executed simultaneously. Various activities were undertaken without waiting for the progress of others to initiate them.

In the area of education, our initial step was to review what had been achieved up to that time. We proposed to lend more prestige to formal education, and for this purpose organized the young people into "social clubs" (*clubes de sociabilización*). We used the term "social clubs" because we intended the clubs to strengthen the friendship ties and solidarity among their members and to facilitate the relations between the individuals and their society. At the same time, we proposed to use these clubs as a way to involve the young people with the educational problems of Kuyo Chico.

We organized two such clubs, one for the males and one for the females. An executive board composed of a president, two captains, and a treasurer was established for the female club, which was then provided with two sewing machines and two sets of kitchen furniture. We set up cooking and sewing programs immediately to stimulate interest among the young women. The girls worked under the direction of a home economics teacher who taught how to cook and sew. Female interest in acquiring these skills, together with the movies and musical programs which were offered and the opportunity to get together and gossip amiably, resulted in various adult women asking to join the club. Schedules were worked out to fit their free periods, and the teacher worked intensely with them. The addition of the adult women brought the need to diversify the club's activities, which branched out into the areas of personal and family hygiene, health care for children, care of the house, cleaning of clothes, and social activities.

The women showed great resistance to the personal hygiene program, particularly with regard to washing the children's clothing. This attitude seems incomprehensible to us, but we must consider the view point of the Indians, who believe that the health and lives of the children are endangered if their clothing is brought into contact, directly or indirectly, with water from the springs where evil spirits dwell. We faced this problem by bringing a parish priest to the town. Before the whole community, the priest said prayers over the springs to exorcise the evil spirits. After this the women were more disposed toward washing clothing and bathing the children.

The male social club was established in a similar manner, emphasizing the men's interest in sports, particularly soccer. A soccer ball was lent to the club by one of the field personnel in the program.

Our interest in organizing these clubs, as we have already noted, rested upon our desire to use them as bases for educational programs involving the adults. This approach was based on the fact that it was the adults of Kuyo Chico who had the power to make decisions concerning community problems. However, as in almost all societies, it is the younger people who have the greatest receptivity to change and innovation, while the older people are characterized by their conservatism, reticence, and resistance to change. For this reason we tried to incorporate as many of the young married men into the club as possible, for in Kuyo Chico a man is considered an adult if he has a woman and heads a family, regardless of how young he may be. Being young, these men would be receptive to the innovations and activities introduced through the club, and, being adults, they would be in a good position to communicate with and influence the older members of the community.

The need for additional equipment became evident as the sports activity of the club grew. The enthusiastic boys desired soccer shoes, a new ball, and uniforms in the club colors to wear in local and regional matches with other teams. Not having the financial means to acquire the new equipment, they decided in one of their club sessions to ask our program for assistance. At first they requested money, which we told them we didn't have. Then, after consultation, Hugo Contreras, the agricultural engineer, told them that they could be helped if they were willing to work very hard, for the only way to raise the money was to cultivate some new fields. This proposal was accepted, and the boys worked very enthusiastically under his direction, ending up with excellent harvests which were sold in town by the women of the female club. These earnings permitted them to buy their equipment and start a club fund.

This fund enabled them to extend their activities later on by renting lands on a neighboring hacienda and planting malting barley for the first time in the region, under an agreement with a brewery (*Compañía Cervecera del Sur del Perú*) which provided a loan of the necessary seed. This project required all the efforts of the agricultural engineer, since the aim of the club was to show an important achievement in the area. The results were clear in a magnificent harvest, both in quantity and quality, and by its own initiative the beer company decided to reward the club with 1.5 U.S. cents per kilo above the market price for their barley. This not only showed what the club was capable of doing, but encouraged the community to initiate the planting of beer barley the following year, having by this time extended the cultivation into several other communities in the area.

In addition to these activities, the members of the club assembled for meetings in a communal room two nights a week. These meetings began with the national anthem and included the reading and explication of paragraphs of the Constitution. On some occasions the content and significance of the statute of communities or of laws related to the Indians were explained. The atmosphere was made pleasant with folk music, and selected films were shown at the end of the meetings, followed by discussions relating to the realities of the local situation. All club decisions were made at these meetings.

We did not wish to start our literacy program in the school immediately, since the adults were not yet convinced that the school wasn't absolutely useless. We decided to launch the project through the social clubs instead, allowing the adults

6. Adult literacy class in new school

to observe the results and form their own conclusions. We wanted to test in practice a hypothesis which I had formulated in 1952, when I was a member of the Andean Indian Mission of the United Nations. In an article entitled "Anthropological and Social Problems of the Andean Region," I wrote the following:

> We believe that the easiest way to teach Indian children to read and write Spanish is to first teach them to write in their own language, using a set of carefully selected words in Quechua or Aymara whose construction and verbalization is such as to be easily and clearly written with the Spanish alphabet. In this way, the children can familiarize themselves with the Spanish alphabet in their own language. Then little by little Spanish words whose learning is made easier by writing them may be introduced to the children. We realize that a special phonetic alphabet developed by linguists is necessary to record accurately the sounds of the Indian languages; however, our aim is not to develop the writing of Quechua or Aymara, but to teach Spanish more efficiently by first teaching the writing of these languages with the Spanish alphabet. In other words, reading and writing in Quechua or Aymara is only a necessary intermediate step toward reading and writing in Spanish."[6]

We believe that the position stated above is justified by the following facts.

1. The previous failures in the country in teaching Indian children to read and write Spanish directly.

2. The previous failures in teaching the reading and writing of Quechua with a special system of writing compatible with the structure of the language.

3. The fact that literacy in Quechua is not important for the Indian in his relations with the Mestizo world.

6. Part of the report of the U.N. Mission, *Informe de la Misión Conjunta de las Naciones Unidas y los Organismos Especializados para el estudio de los problemas de las poblaciones indígenas andinas*, prepared for the governments of Bolivia, Peru and Ecuador (Geneva, 1953), pp. 105–37. The same article appeared in the review of the University of Cuzco for the first semester of 1953. See *Revista Universitaria del Cuzco*, no. 104, pp. 272–320.

It is a fact that monolinguism goes hand in hand with illiteracy; therefore, it is necessary to deal with both problems simultaneously. According to the system we proposed, an individual would learn an unknown skill—the use of an alphabet or writing—on the foundation of previous knowledge—his mother tongue, the language in which he normally expresses himself. When the individual can write words in his own language, he has a broader base of knowledge to serve as a foundation for his learning of a new unknown—the Spanish language. In this way there is a gradual progression from the native language through writing to the new language.

Rodolfo Sánchez Castañeda, the educator in the program, in collaboration with the anthropologist, was charged with the preparation of two primers to be used in the literacy project. To facilitate the learning of the five vowels in the Spanish alphabet, we decided to associate each of the letters with something whose Quechua name began with that vowel sound. Thus we made drawings of a falcon (*Anca*) for the letter "A," a place where grain is threshed (*Era*) for the letter "E," the sun (*Inti*) for the letter "I," etc. Then the vowels were combined with consonants to form syllables, which were combined to construct Quechua words accompanied by more drawings. The first primer, forty-two pages long, was later published in Quechua under the title *Ñahuinchista Quicharisun*—"Let Us Open Our Eyes."[7] The second primer, forty-four pages long, was structured in a similar way and published in Spanish with the title *Sigamos Leyendo*—"Let Us Continue Reading."[8]

Literacy groups were formed with people ranging in age from fourteen to thirty, with those not belonging to the clubs allowed to register. Taking into account the daily work schedule of the *peasants* as well as the yearly agricultural calendar,

7. Oscar Núñez del Prado and Rodolfo Sánchez C., *Ñahuinchista Quicharisun*. System of Alphabetization of the Native Language. Ministry of Labor and Indian Affairs. National Plan for the Integration of the Indian Population (Lima, Peru, 1964).

8. Oscar Núñez del Prado and Rodolfo Sánchez C., *Sigamos Leyendo*. Global Simultaneous Method of Reading and Writing. Ministry of Labor and Indian Affairs. National Plan for Integration (Lima, Peru, 1965).

we decided to modify the official school year to encompass the period from November to April.[9] Classes were held three times a week and lasted for two hours each. Since the Indians normally go to sleep shortly after sunset, around 7:00 p.m., and rise early, between 5:30 and 6:00 a.m., we decided to schedule the classes for the period between 5:00 and 8:00 a.m. The actual lesson ran from 5:30 to 7:30, which allowed them a half hour before going to work, which they usually began at 8:00 a.m.

During the first two years of the project, Professor Sánchez dedicated himself personally to the application of our method of instruction, using the primers we had written. Although the announced age limit for the classes was thirty, several older members of the community solicited admission shortly after the program began and were accepted, among them the cabecilla, who was then forty-five, and at this writing is personero.[10]

In 1962, one boy and one girl from Kuyo Chico were trained to be instructors who would use the same method, and a small group of monolingual and illiterate adults was turned over to them. In the male group Francisco Mamani Jiwaña succeeded in teaching three out of six adults to read and write, while in the female group, Fidelia Díaz Kispe was successful with four out of the five women involved.

During this initial period we could not count on any assistance from the other teachers in the area, as they bore us much ill will. They viewed our presence as the introduction of undesirable controls, since we put an end to many of the abuses which the Indians had suffered regularly at their hands. They were accustomed to conducting their affairs in an irregular manner, and it was usual for them to begin the school week on Monday afternoon or Tuesday, then leave on Friday to return to the city; furthermore, they often took advantage of the allowance for sick leave and went off on prolonged ab-

9. The official school year for Peru runs from late March or early April to late December.
10. Legally recognized representative of an official Indian community, elected solely by the members of the community.

sences. We simply demanded that they attend to their labors regularly and treat the Indians with some degree of consideration and respect.

Another factor concerning the attitudes of these teachers was the fact that they were directly subordinate to the Ministry of Education and did not want to feel tied to our program in any way, viewing it as something which might limit their autonomy. Despite the fact that the presidential decree which had created the National Plan for Integration included as a primary institution the Ministry of Education, we were almost never able to obtain the collaboration of the local office of the ministry. On the contrary, the educational authorities seemed to think that we should function without aid or authority. Our requests for qualified personnel to help us were ignored, or else persons would be sent who had been dismissed from other schools for disciplinary reasons, old age, or incompetence.

In some of the other schools in the area the teachers attempted to discredit our program. We recall one instance in which we were using X-ray machines in a campaign to eradicate tuberculosis. One of the teachers in a nearby area sent emissaries to the various communities to spread the word that we were foreign agents who had been sent to change the Indian race. For this purpose we were using sterilizing machines on the men, with the aim of later bringing North American breeders to fertilize the Indian women.

The programs of study which we followed in the Kuyo Chico school were the same as those used in other Peruvian schools at the corresponding level, due to the national educational regulations. Standardized plans of study and required hours of attendance could not be altered, nor could the official school year, running from March to December. However, it was possible to introduce methodological changes and innovations, such as our method of teaching Spanish, and some types of activities which, though not officially required, might enrich the school life of the children, such as small agricultural and workshop projects.

The success of our methodological innovations in the adult

literacy program brought a greater attendance of children in the school, since the adults, seeing for themselves the results of their studies, began to feel that it might be worthwhile to send their children to school. This led to an interesting mechanism of repercussion. As a result of our adult literacy program, more children attended the school, where they learned about agricultural practices which they conveyed to their families, influencing the adults to start planting more family gardens.

Serious attention to the school program required the acquisition of additional teaching materials and more adequate teaching space, and in 1960 we set out to complete the new school building which the community had started to build earlier. The walls were stuccoed. Metal window frames with glass panes were installed. A flat ceiling was constructed along with concrete floors. Wall blackboards and toilet facilities were provided and the building was painted. An additional effort obtained desks from the Office of Education in Calca.

Later on, we suggested that the community build a comfortable house for the teachers to live in. As communal property, the rent from the house could go into the community fund. The suggestion met with approval, and construction began, being completed in early 1964. Before the building could serve its intended purpose, a problem arose: shifting of the land upon which the school building was erected had resulted in dangerous cracks in the walls of two rooms. It was necessary to tear down part of this building for safety, leaving only one room. Part of the school operations were transferred to the building which had been built for the teachers, and the rest to the building erected for the bread factory. The recovery of the lands which the church had owned has opened the possibility of building a new school, and to date the foundation has been excavated for a building large enough to meet present and future needs.

We have indicated that, upon our arrival in Kuyo Chico, the school was a primary school, with one teacher handling all three grades. In 1961 we obtained authorization from the

Ministry of Education to begin conducting second-level studies, although not even one new teacher was appointed to assist
us. We began a program of three-year studies with seven students, but were unable to continue it in 1962, for the enroll-
ment in the transition grade had grown, and one teacher was
unable to handle all four grades alone (transition, first, second,
and third). The assistance of a teacher from the Peace Corps,
Dolores Aguayo, enabled us to resume the third-year program
in 1963, and the first graduating class of the second level left
the school in 1965. From this point on, the number of teachers
working in the school went up to three.

School attendance continued to rise until 1966, and has
been relatively stable at 155 to 160 students since then. This
is due to the fact that practically all of the eligible children
in the three communities which the Kuyo Chico school serves
now attend school, making Kuyo Chico the only school in the
province of Calca to drive away the phantom of school absenteeism. In addition, there has been some attendance by
children from more distant communities, such as Amphay
(four male students in 1964, eight in 1965, two in 1966), Kulis-
pata (one in 1964, one in 1966), Paru Paru (five in 1966) and
Qotokaki (five in 1966). Since 1966, the attendance of children from these far-off communities has continued to grow;
in 1967 and 1968, there were even two boys from Mandorpujio
in the province of Paucartambo, approximately forty kilometers away.

It should be mentioned that there were some students from
Kuyo Chico, Qotobamba, and Mask'a who attended the Central Indian School in Pisaq, perhaps because that school was
well staffed with teachers and supervisors, whereas in Kuyo
Chico three teachers had to handle all six grades. On the other
hand, it may be that the parents desired their children to be
in schools which they considered bigger and better.

The following attendance chart indicates two interesting
facts: first, the rate of growth of the student body in general
and, second, the growing tendency to send girls to school,
something very uncommon in rural Peru.

Concerning adult literacy, the system we employed has

	1960		1961		1962		1963		1964		1965		1966	
	M	F	M	F	M	F	M	F	M	F	M	F	M	F
Transition	18	8	25	20	33	26	24	20	26	29	25	23	29	16
First year	12	3	9	7	14	8	15	7	19	12	18	13	19	22
Second year	8	1	8	3	6	5	9	6	8	6	11	8	11	6
Third year	—	—	5	2	—	—	6	5	10	4	7	2	11	9
Fourth year	—	—	—	—	—	—	—	—	—	—	6	3	8	3
Subtotals	38	12	47	32	53	39	54	38	63	51	67	49	78	56
Total attendance	50		79		92		92		114		116		134	

produced significant results. In the first program of 1961–62, sixteen out of twenty-five students learned to read and write in six months, with three two-hour classes a week. These classes were continued, with similar results, through 1965 in Kuyo Chico and several neighboring communities. The educator in charge, Rodolfo Sánchez Castañeda, makes the following comments upon the "native language" method I proposed in 1952:

> Tests of this method have been conducted both within and outside the republic. It was used at the Summer Institute of Linguistics in Peru in 1954, and was also employed by the linguist and educator Ethel Emilia Wallis working with a group of monolingual Indians in the region of Cakchiquel, through the collaboration of the *Instituto Indigenista* of Guatamala and the Summer Institute of Linguistics.
>
> The most important Peruvian experience was that of Maria Asunción Galindo at the *Escuela Pedagogica de Ojherani* in Puno, who achieved bilinguism quickly and efficiently by teaching the *aymarans* of the region to first read and write in their own language.[11]

Little by little the teachers in Kuyo Chico became interested in the method, and eventually its application extended to various schools within the sphere of influence of the Central Peasant School of Pisaq, whose literacy classes were staffed by volunteer teachers. The use of the two primers

11. From "Organización de Neuve Comunidades Indígenas de la Província de Calca," report of the *Instituto Indigenista Peruano,* 1966.

which had been printed by the Plan for Integration also spread, until more than one thousand children in the area received these as texts in school, and thus benefitted from our program. The second volume has also been used with satisfactory results by various teachers in the province of Calca. Yet despite the high volume of requests for more texts from many schools in the province, the Institute was unable to provide the funds necessary for another printing.

At present the teachers at the Kuyo Chico school feel satisfied with their work. The program has done everything possible to contribute to the love and pride they feel for the school. For example, vehicles belonging to the program were used to bring the floats which had been prepared by teachers and children for the elaborately celebrated Spring Festivals to Pisaq to participate in the festivities. The Kuyo Chico soccer team won the district championship, in competition with all the other communities in the area, including Pisaq. In addition, the children of Kuyo Chico did very well on the aptitude and achievement tests administered under the auspices of the Central School of Pisaq.

The community education program has had many good effects. In 1963, a survey showed that illiteracy had been lowered by 18 percent in the three communities of Kuyo Chico, Qotobamba, and Mask'a. Although no later survey has been conducted, we believe that this reduction has increased to between 25 and 30 percent. About thirty students have graduated from the primary school of Kuyo Chico, and the majority of these are either in the new secondary school which has opened in Tambowaqso, Pisaq, or else in the national schools of Cuzco. Some of them are continuing agricultural study in the Calca school. At least four youths from the community are now agricultural technicians, and two have traveled to Wisconsin in the United States and are now working in government programs in Peru. One youth pursued nursing training in Cuzco, and two have become masons, two chauffeurs, two carpenters, and one a tailor.

The literacy classes also provided us with the opportunity to introduce agricultural, health, and citizenship education, thus preparing the peasants for a greater participation in the Mestizo world. The possibility of obtaining a voting card (*libreta electoral*) was a great incentive, and with the political campaign of 1962 came their first opportunity to participate in the national elections. Of the ninety-one people who had learned to read and write, sixty presented themselves for registration at Pisaq. The judge did everything he could think of to disqualify them, finally giving them a test involving grammar and writing which even the members of the judging board could not have passed. Even so, twenty-eight men and two women were approved, received their voting cards, and participated in the election.

During the literacy classes there had been some instruction concerning procedures to be followed at the elections, allowing also for the possibility that one of the students might be chosen by lot from all registered voters to serve as poll watcher. When the election came, one of the Indians was chosen to be president of one of the polling places in Pisaq. The governor, the mayor, the judge, and the police chief all tried to veto the designation, but we were present and saw to it that they abided by the results of the lottery, as prescribed by law. When they tried to claim that an Indian could not preside over one of the polling places because he was not capable of doing it, we simply invited them to look over the election law, which says that if a citizen has not shown incapacity in the exercise of the function, no veto could be exercised against him. The authorities had to accept the situation, and the Indian presided at one of the precincts, executing his duty flawlessly. It is not an exaggeration to say that the Mestizos who voted in that precinct during the election viewed with repugnance the signature on their voting cards, of an Indian who presided over the polling place to which they had come in compliance with their civic duty.

Health—The New Role of the Doctor

We began our health program with Dr. Rigoberto Dávila Aguirre. I had first met Dr. Dávila in 1958, when I was responsible for executing a field study in the department of Cuzco under the auspices of the SCIPS (*Servicio Cooperativo Interamericano del Plan del Sur*). In March of that year I arrived in the jungle region of Q'Osñipata, where a medical post functioned under the direction of Dr. Dávila. He was a young professional man, full of enthusiasm and energy, and immersed joyfully in an extraordinary range of activities, considering that he lacked adequate facilities and supplies and was relatively immobile in an extensive area with a scattered population and a host of diseases and dangers. We had the opportunity to discuss casually the applied anthropology project, which at that time was already before the Indian Institute. When I explained what I proposed to do, he expressed interest in working in such a program. I agreed to call him when the program was under way, and he was free of other commitments. In this way, he eventually came to join the group working on the Kuyo Chico project.

This group was totally dedicated from the start. The doctor entered the program enthusiastically, understanding completely its nature and aims. We discussed strategies, and decided that it would be best for him to begin working with the native healers (*curanderos*), that is, to assist them, and to take advantage of this opportunity to observe their practices: to see how they identified and treated diseases, and to what causes they attributed the diseases. In this way he would become familiar with customary procedures before and during medical treatment, and also gain the trust and confidence of the curanderos. He was free to intervene in some cases, but only to offer advice or consult with the curandero, not to interfere with the treatment. Once he had learned the names given to various illnesses, he could prescribe medicines, indicating that they were especially made to treat these diseases. For example, he would indicate that antibiotics were especially good for treating *mal de Soq'a* (tuberculosis), or the sulfa drugs for *el Pujiu* (gastrointestinal infections), trying to associate these drugs with the various earths, shell scrapings, and other materials which the Indians prescribe. Proceeding in this way, he gradually gained the confidence of

7. Native healer setting arm in cast

the entire community, including the curanderos, who began to initiate consultations with him.

Dr. Dávila was able to obtain much information concerning the causes assigned to illnesses by the Indians. These fall into three main categories: natural, supernatural, and mixed. In the natural category are such illnesses as colds (*chiriq atisqan*), sore throats (*q'oni*), and thrush, a children's mouth infection (*sonqophatku*), which can be treated solely with herbs, fruits, and mineral substances, and do not require the participation of spirits or occult forces. The second category includes all diseases caused by the direct intervention of spirits, such as tuberculosis (*soq'a*), pneumonia (*pachaq-hap'isqan*), and cyrrosis (*k'uychi*). The third category includes diseases which are caused by natural factors with the assistance of spirits. For example, rickets (*mancharisqa*), which affects the young, is caused when a child falls and the earth takes over his spirit. Certain allergies (*isu-wayra*) are caused by the winds, which is interesting to note, since in actuality allergic reactions are caused by some substances which can be carried by winds. We should mention a fourth type of illness, which is caused by natural forces or fluids. No supernatural spirits are involved here, but some animals can have these powers, which instill a profound fear (*Q'aqcha*) in the victim. Except for the first category, the treatment of all these illnesses involves some magic. The intervention of specialists is required to diagnose these illnesses by way of dreams, the reading of the heated urine (*qollpasqa*), divination (*wish-ch'uy*), or the conjuring of the mountain spirits. Only the illnesses of the first variety can be diagnosed directly through observation of the symptoms.

There are also prophylactic measures practiced by the Indians, consisting of the ingestion of medicinal beverages to prevent some illnesses, or more general precautions against all ills. The *qespillo* are fruits of the bean plant, which fall from the plant but survive for some time without being destroyed or eaten by animals. These receive a spell from a *brujo* (sorcerer) and are turned over to individuals to ward off evils. The *walqha* are small bags filled with special preparations and tied to children to protect them. *Lloq'esqa* are made from twisted wools of various animals, and are tied to the heels or wrists to prevent certain illnesses.

We considered it important to surround the doctor with an aura of prestige. One opportunity to do this arose in October 1959, during our campaign to eradicate tuberculosis, when we had an X-ray machine at our disposal. Using a dark room in one of the *peasant* homes, we were able to give 352 people X-ray examinations. We had ten to fifteen people enter the room simultaneously, so that while one person passed by the screen, the others could observe the way in which the doctor was able to examine the inside of the body. They were left confounded and full of respect and admiration when they learned that the doctor could see the heart, lungs, and bones in this way. Whether or not they related this to the supernatural, it is clear that, from that point on, they attributed very special powers to the doctor, whose respect and prestige grew in the surrounding communities as well.

Later, in one of the assemblies, we announced that we had set up a medical post where people could come to see the doctor for treatment of common ills such as skin irritations, injuries, headaches, and stomach aches. Little by little, the number of patients treated at the post increased, and soon patients were coming from such distant communities as Warkhi, Pillawara, and Lamay. By the end of 1959, 233 patients had been seen, with the following geographical distribution: Pillawara, San Salvador, Taray, Lamay, Amaru, and Paru Paru, 1 each; Chango and Warki, 2 each; Qoya y Makay, 5; Qotobamba, 15; Kuyo Grande and Mask'a, 26 each; Amphay, 34; Pisaq, 43; and Kuyo Chico, 72.

Almost all of the program's personnel were released at the end of that year, including the doctor, because of a national austerity program. For more than a year, the secretary who had been assigned to us by the university and fortunately knew something about nursing had to run the medical post, until the crisis passed and we were able to hire another doctor, who resigned after seven months.

Dr. Victor Guillén Lorena assumed the position of doctor

from June 1962 on. He had excellent qualifications for the job, being not only a capable doctor but also a man able to gain the confidence of the people. Dr. Guillén established many close friendships with the *peasants* and even with the Mestizos of Pisaq.

Although the program had been in existence for several years at that point, there was still one area which doctors had not been able to penetrate: prenatal care and childbirth. However, a fortuitous event enabled the doctor to participate in this area: a case of transverse delivery arose, in which the baby's hand was presented first and the curandero proclaimed that delivery was impossible and that both mother and child would die. In consultation with the anthropologist, the doctor proposed to take the woman to the hospital in Cuzco as a last resort. It was necessary to consult with the family, of course, for according to local beliefs it is very undesirable to be buried far from the community. We promised to return the woman's body in case of her death, and to pay for the funeral. This proposal was accepted, and we were able to rush the woman to the hospital in a station wagon. Though the baby could not be saved, fifteen days later the doctor returned with a healthy mother, and the final barrier had been broken. The doctor had won the respect of the *peasants* for modern medicine.

Once the doctor had access to childbirth, a small problem arose: no child had a layette prepared beforehand, for it was believed that a child for whom clothes were made in advance would either die or cause the death of the mother. To resolve this difficulty, a cooperative was organized from the women in the social club to make layettes. Since the clothes were being prepared by the cooperative and were not designated for any particular child, there was no danger involved, and the layette could be acquired by the family shortly after the birth of the child.

Although it took over four years, scientific medicine has now been accepted in the Indian communities, though this does not mean that curanderos, magic, and traditional practices have been abandoned. The curanderos have retained their prestige and are considered indispensable for the treatment of dislocations or bone fractures, since they know how to make splints and casts. Also, all illnesses caused by supernatural spirits are still turned over to specialists, for they are considered beyond the competence of the doctor. This makes some sense, for witchcraft involves the psychological treatment of certain illnesses. For example, a session with the *Alto-misayoq,* in which the Apus present themselves in bubbles of the heated urine (*collpasqa*) to diagnose the illness, can have a tremendous effect on the mental health of the patient, for the curandero understands very well the psychological factors which affect the personalities of the Indians.

The Peasant Hospital

Despite the effectiveness of our health program, many complications arose. Many patients required prolonged treatment or hospital facilities, and we had to use our influence to get them accepted into the Antonio Lorena Hospital in Cuzco, as they are usually denied admission because of their inability to pay the hospital fees or because of lack of adequate facilities to accommodate them. A stay in the city hospital is very uncomfortable for the *Indian,* who is far from his community and family in a strange environment, with unfamiliar objects, strange food, and no one who speaks his language. The city hospital is designed for people of a different cultural extraction. To these problems we must add the disrespectful and sometimes hostile treatment which the Indian receives from the Mestizos. We have heard Indians tell of being systematically turned away from hospitals when they asked to see a doctor; in some cases, people who have been denied medical attention have died on their way back to the community.

This situation made us consider the possibility of establishing a hospital for the *peasants* of the region, specifically tailored to their needs and cultural background.

In 1963 we contacted representatives of the World Health Organization and the International Labor Organization, and they secured for us a donation from the Swiss canton of

Geneva, which included beds, sterilizing equipment, medical and surgical instruments, and a mobile unit to serve as a mobile doctor's office. In addition, the National Plan for Integration obtained for us an appropriation from the Ministry of Labor and Indian Affairs for the acquisition of those construction materials which could not be supplied by the communities involved in the project. The National Plan also secured an agreement with *Cooperación Popular,* the government community-development agency, whereby its architects would draw up the plans for the hospital and provide us with technical assistance.

A major problem still remained. We had obtained the necessary resources to build the hospital, but did not have the land to put it on, for as we have already indicated, there was a suffocating shortage of land in Kuyo Chico. For this reason we negotiated with the Convent of Santo Domingo in Cuzco to acquire the necessary land from the nearby hacienda in Sañuwasi, which they owned. The convent agreed to make a donation of one hectare of land next to the Kuyo Chico road, in a place called Matará. This was on April 29, 1965.

It happened, however, that the representative of a group of capitalist agriculturalists who rented the Sañuwasi property from the convent opposed this donation, pointing to an agreement which they had with the convent granting them the option of buying the land. He suggested that land in a different location, Qollpapampa, be donated to us. This location is far from the road and extremely inaccessible, as a gigantic boulder and eucalyptus woods make it impossible to build a road there. Furthermore, it was located on the bank of a river which completely flooded the area when it ran high. Finally, a set of conditions was proposed for the donation. The hacienda was not going to provide water or right of way, and the peasants were to be required to build an adobe wall for security purposes. The wall was to be more than 500 meters long, and the peasants had the option of erecting a barbed wire fence, within three months and at their own expense (about 50,000 *soles*), until the wall could be built. Following these proposals, the convent informed us on May 25 that our earlier agreement had been nullified. Refusing to accept the terms of the new proposal, we were thus unable to build the hospital in this area.

Dr. Pelegrín Román, director of the Plan for Integration, knowing of our difficulties, obtained an appropriation for us to purchase some land from a neighboring Mestizo. A contract was drawn up and the money turned over, but we were not able to complete the agreement because of the way in which the land was divided. Thus we had to look elsewhere once again.

Many years earlier, the Indians had been thrown off some lands by a neighboring hacendado. They took this case to court, and we spoke to the judicial board, who granted us one hectare of the land under dispute. Having accomplished this, we went to see the hacendado who held the land, and told him that the community was going to donate it for a public project. At first he was indignant, claiming that the land belonged to him and that the Indians had no right to donate it. After some discussion of our point of view, however, he offered to donate the necessary land, and we sealed the agreement. At last there was nothing left to do but start the work.

An assembly was called, in which it was agreed to ask the help of all those communities interested in the construction of a hospital. The personero sent offcial letters to twenty-two communities, inviting them to send representatives to an intercommunity assembly on a specific date, to arrange participation in the work. One hundred thirty delegates arrived for the assembly, including mayors, cabecillas, personeros and other officials. The assembly established an Intercommunity Board of Peasant Development, which immediately held elections to select a board of directors, including a president, vice president, secretary, treasurer, auditor, and four board members. The personero of Kuyo Chico was elected president, and the other positions went to representatives from Amphay, Pisaq, Kuyo Chico, Pillawara, Kuyo Grande, Qoya-runa, Chawaytirí, and Qotobamba. The board set to work at once to plan the organization of the work, and there was almost a dispute about which community should have the honor of heading the list of towns in the work schedule. The delegate from Kuyo Chico wanted his town to be first, since they were the community originally involved in the project, while the representative from Pisaq claimed that his town should be first, since it was the principal community in the district. Finally it was agreed that Pisaq would head the list, with the other towns drawing lots to establish their order. In this way a schedule of work shifts was established, and the communities committed themselves to sending a certain number of workers on the designated days.

Leonard Choquetinco, the foreman of the program, was to direct the work, with the assistance of Antenor Olivera Araujo, who was to maintain contact with the participating communities. Work was assigned, including the removal of stones, leveling of the ground, and carrying of lumber, sand, and gravel. Some of the communities, including Paru Paru, Viacha, and Chawaytirí, took the responsibility for providing the straw necessary for the adobes. On the opening day of each community's shift, the peasants arrived carrying the national flag and accompanied by musicians who played throughout the day's work.

In July 1965 we obtained the use of a tractor for eight days from *Cooperación Popular,* agreeing to pay the salaries of the driver and his helper and the costs of the gasoline and oil required. This enabled us to clear and level land for the first room of the hospital. In October of the same year we again requested the use of the tractor, but our request was denied. After this, the only assistance we could get from the *Cooperación Popular* was the planning and surveying of the first wing by one of their engineers. The work proceeded completely under the direction of the foreman, Choquetinco.

Despite the enthusiasm of the peasants, there were periods in which they were unable to work on the project because they had to attend to the planting and harvesting of their crops. It should be noted that the Indians did not receive any salary or payment for their work. There were only two salaried workmen, both artisans.

Early in 1967 the first wing was roofed. This wing included a waiting room, pharmacy, storage room, examination room, treatment room, and delivery room. The rest of the year was used to paint and install the doors, windows, flat ceiling, stucco, and electricity. Today a medical post operates in this building, directed by the sanitation specialist of the program.

In 1968 we began a second wing, and upon its completion began a third, destined to serve as a residence for the doctor and staff. A fourth wing is planned, to serve as a temporary residence for the families of patients (*tambo*).

In April 1966, Dr. Guillen left his post to go abroad, and shortly thereafter a government order froze all positions, so that we were unable to obtain a replacement. Since then the program has remained without a doctor. The sanitation specialist has taken charge of the medical post, providing treatment there as well as making house calls to neighboring communities at all hours of the day and night, and bringing more serious cases to the Antonio Lorena Hospital in Cuzco. But the absence of a doctor has discouraged the peasants, and attendance for work on the hospital has diminished markedly. However, the medical attention which has been given to the Mestizos at Kuyo Chico, as well as personal relations between the personnel of the program and the Mestizos in the town, has brought about better relations with the Mestizos of the area, to the extent that many of them come of their own initiative to help carry out the project.

Religion

We did not propose to carry out any projects organized around religion. It seemed to us that religion was a very delicate area to work in, since any activity on our part, such as an attempt to introduce or clarify Catholic concepts, would cast us as missionaries in the eyes of the Indians. If we proceeded in this manner, the Indians would believe that we were tied to the interests of the parish church, which had taken their lands; yet if we assumed a position opposing the church, it would affirm the parish position, namely, that the members of the Kuyo Chico program were communists and enemies of God. Thus we decided to refrain from getting involved in this area.

We aided the peasants in any way possible whenever help was requested, whether for transportation into town to attend mass or hold a baptism, or for use of the microphones and amplifier during First Communion ceremonies. The program did not sponsor any religious activities itself, except for one occasion when there was no other alternative available. Nevertheless, we continued to be deeply bothered by the role which Catholic celebrations played in draining the Indian economy, particularly the mechanism of assigning cargos, which all but ruined many families.[12]

The problem had to be faced in some way, so finally we decided to try to use our influence in the community to alter the situation. At some of the assemblies, we expressed the belief that it was good to worship God and the saints, but that they would not look with pleasure upon the fact that, in order to do so, some people had to sell lands left to them by ancestors, or make their children live in constant hunger. In this and private conversations, it seemed that our point of view was being accepted, until finally the personero of the community, who was the next person charged with a cargo, became convinced that "to stay on good terms with God" it was only necessary to join in the celebration of mass. He feared criticism from those who had already accepted cargos in the past, as it is these people who are most likely to desire that others not escape the obligation. When the scheduled day arrived, the personero arranged to have a mass celebrated and offered some refreshments afterwards, indicating that his obligations ended there. A few people protested weakly, but it seems that everyone had secretly hoped that someone would have the courage to break with tradition.

12. See "The Spiritual World" in chapter 2 above. On the costs of the fiesta system, see H. and T. E. Castillo and A. Reville, *Carcas, The Forgotten Community* (Cornell University, Department of Anthropology, 1964).

We do not know whether it was the prestige of Tomás Díaz and the respect which the community had for him which prevented the matter from becoming serious, or whether the people really came to see how harmful the tradition had been. In an assembly held in October 1968, someone asked to be excused from a responsibility which had been assigned to him, claiming that he was unable to carry it out because he still had a cargo to perform in Qoyllurit'i. One of the young community members stated that not only had many people been financially ruined because of the cargos, but they also have held back the progress of the community by being unable to meet their obligations. He then proposed that cargos be abolished and that the position of *arariwa* be established. The arariwas were to have general care of the crops, protecting them from damage by animals, to see that the water for irrigation was not wasted, and to check on attendance at the community work projects or *waykas*. Various speakers supported the motion, including Tomás Díaz. A vote was then taken, and the proposal passed unanimously. The person who held the cargo in Qoyllurit'i asked that he be allowed to carry it out, since he had already committed himself to it. His request was granted, after which elections were held to select the first three arariwas.

Relations between the parish and the peasants were intense, revolving around the central celebrations, such as baptisms, marriages, and funerals. During the first years of the program, a campaign against us from the pulpit caused considerable difficulties for us in our relations with the Indians. However, it would not have been wise to confront this power directly, so we waited for a convenient opportunity to improve our standing with the parish priest. We enlisted the aid of one of the best student musical groups in Cuzco—friends of ours—to go and serenade the priest on his birthday. Courtesy required that he open his doors to us after such an obvious display of friendship. We conversed amicably, taking advantage of the cordial atmosphere to discuss tactfully the program of applied anthropology. Afterwards, the priest discontinued his campaign against us.

Chapter Three

Some Failures

The program also experienced some failures. In one of the project team meetings, the doctor pointed out the advantages of raising the fireplaces off the floor, to make cooking safer and more hygienic. By placing the fireplace three feet off the ground, contamination of the food by the children's playing or by contact with the earth could be avoided. In addition, this change would eliminate the existing danger of a child being severely burned by the hot coals or scalded by boiling water.

On Saturday, during a community assembly, I abruptly proposed the benefits of raising the fireplaces, citing the reasons just mentioned. The community did not oppose this plan; in fact, someone said, in effect, "If you think that it would be good to do this, then we will do it right away." Teams were formed and began work the following Monday, going from house to house and constructing fireplaces according to plans they had been given. The work continued for some time, and 142 new fireplaces were constructed in the communities of Kuyo Chico, Qotobamba, and Mask'a.

The work having been completed, we forgot about the matter, until some time later we decided to check on the results of these changes. We went from house to house, and to our great surprise discovered that only 3 of the 142 fireplaces were in use. This disturbed us, and we investigated to find out why our project had failed. We discovered three main reasons. First, it is believed that for a woman to be a good housewife, she must surround herself with everything she needs to prepare the foods, then sit down next to the fire and not rise again until the meal is ready. Second, the Indians believe that the woman should keep the heat and cinders of the fire from hitting her stomach, as this dries up the womb, either making her sterile or resulting in a very difficult pregnancy and possibly a fatal delivery. Third, the preparation of the food is often turned over to the young daughters, who require special arrangements in order to move the pots around. In addition, the children like to go over to the fireplace and take portions of hot *mote* (corn mush) from the pots. For all these reasons, a fireplace situated on the floor is better suited to their needs. As the anthropologist, I had completely failed to understand these factors. The responsibility was exclusively mine, for the job of the anthropologist was to decide how to introduce changes based on an understanding of the Indian culture. In this particular case, I had neglected to consider some important factors.

On another occasion, we obtained a donation of ten breeding rams, with which we planned to improve the sheep stock in Kuyo Chico, Qotobamba, and Mask'a. This did not arouse the enthusiasm which we expected, for herds in the community were so small that it was not worth the trouble of taking care of the breeders. In addition, the new rams were accustomed to higher altitudes and did not adapt well to Kuyo Chico, and their presence logically involved the elimination of the male sheep previously owned. Thus we had to take back the rams and send them to some distant communities in the highlands where they were really useful and appreciated by the people.

A third case concerned the cultivation of potatoes, which we wanted to introduce in the community. In 1963 the agricultural engineer organized a cooperative to work a piece of land ceded by one of the members of the community. The people had no previous experience of this kind and had to obtain potatoes for planting by bartering with the high communities, exchanging corn for the potatoes. These were planted, and after the earth was mounded around them, I noticed that the furrows were too deep, so that, in my judgment, the roots of the plant would remain on the surface and would not be able to grow and yield a harvest. I expressed my concern to the agricultural engineer, but he replied that modern techniques have demonstrated that potatoes grow well even with deep furrows. By all accounts, he was the agricultural expert, not I. Yet when the long-awaited harvest came, it did not even cover the amount of seed planted. The community became discouraged about the possibility of potato planting in the area.

Two years later, the foreman of the program, Leonard Choquetinco, decided to make a test of his own, for which he rented some land from the community. The people were skeptical about this project, but when it appeared that the harvest might be good, they accepted an invitation to help gather it. The results were excellent, and using newly available lands, the people now have a large potato cooperative, which promises to be very successful.

In conclusion, we may say that of the three failures which we had, two were due to technical reasons and the third was due to the failure to take into account cultural factors of great importance.

The Reorganization of the Community

A community which is not officially recognized has no legal protection and is totally at the mercy of the local Mestizos, who can expropriate Indian lands through many devious schemes, including the forging of documents (which usually hold up in court). On the other hand, the law establishes that the lands of recognized communities cannot be alienated, mortgaged, loaned, or given as security, and that the rights with respect to the lands are inalienable.

Nevertheless, there are still many Indian communities which are not officially recognized, because the necessary prerequisites may be too difficult for the community to manage: for example, the presentation of maps showing the boundaries of the community, a census of the population according to sex and age, and an inventory of the cattle and crops belonging to each community member. Given the economic condition of the Indians, it is very difficult for them to contract an engineer to survey the boundaries of the town, and the widespread illiteracy makes it practically impossible for them to take the census themselves, following the required official procedures. Although the communities are generally interested in obtaining legal recognition, the circumstances are such that it is usually not possible for them to do so.

Among the unrecognized communities in which we were conducting our program, two types of local governmental structure can be distinguished: the first, corresponding to Kuyo Chico, Qotobamba, and Mask'a, is headed by a cabecilla, while the second, corresponding to Amaru and Kuyo Grande, is headed by a chief mayor (*envarado*) and a series of *segundas, regidores* and *alguaciles*. We have already indicated how these officials were completely subordinate to the Mestizo authorities of the district capital, who basically made use of them as servants or as objects of abuse.

It seemed indispensable that the community obtain legal recognition and, in so doing, neutralize the political power of the Mestizo authorities. No action could be more effective in achieving this end than to establish a new form of government in the community, one which would not be subordinated to the Mestizos but would instead express the will of the Indians in the communities. There already existed laws which could be of use to us in this task. Laws nos. 605 and 479 abolish the position of envarado along with other types of political servants, and the Statute of Communities of 1928, together with the Supreme Decrees of July 18, 1938, and January 13, 1941, recognize the authority of the personeros and directive boards in community self-government.

We made a formal promise to help the community follow the procedures required to obtain legal recognition. This stimulated the interest of the Indians in this matter, and their collaboration opened many doors for us. First of all, it made it easier for us to administer the questionnaires which we needed for our research, for this could be done along with the registration and census required for recognition. Secondly, in addition to strengthening the good feelings of the peasants towards our program, it enabled us to organize a governing board composed of elected representatives from the community, for the law states that to initiate proceedings a community must elect representatives under the supervision of authorities from the Office of Indian Affairs (now the Office of Communities). This board started functioning before any action had been taken on the application for recognition, and we knew that from then on any activities which we organized would be closely tied to this board.

A personero, secretary, and treasurer would represent the community before the Ministry of Labor and Indian Affairs during the procedure to obtain recognition. In addition to these positions, the governing board was to have an auditor and a fifth member.

On the date specified by the Inspector of Indian Affairs of Calca, the community was called together for a general assembly to elect the governing board. All of the adults were present, both male and female, and in order to eliminate the possibility of social or familial pressures, a secret ballot was decided on. A voting booth and ballot box had to be improvised for the occasion.

The community was asked to nominate candidates, and the nominees were identified by placing pieces of colored paper in the hat bands. We explained to the assembly that each voter would receive some pieces of paper, matching the identifying colors of the candidates. After making sure that he had all of the necessary slips of paper, the voter would proceed to the booth, where he was to deposit in the ballot box the slip with the color of the candidate to whom he wanted to give his vote, and then discard the unused pieces of paper into a box placed on the floor. This explanation was repeated several times, to make sure that everyone understood the voting procedure.

Tomás Díaz Qhapa and his maternal brother, Francisco Becerra Qhapa, who also was well-respected in the community, were nominated for the position of personero. The voting proceeded slowly, with the women in particular seeming very indecisive. When the balloting was completed, the ballot box was opened before the entire community, and the slips of paper grouped according to color and then counted aloud. The winner was Tomás Díaz, who was immediately proclaimed personero. The assembly proceeded to elect the other board members in the same manner, completing the installation of the first governing board in the presence of the Inspector of Indian Affairs.

Although the board legally represented the community, ultimate authority is still vested in the community assembly. In the beginning, the board met every two weeks in the communal hall, assisted by a member of the program, to decide upon what was to be brought up at the monthly assembly. The assembly was presided over by the personero, assisted by one of the program personnel, and deliberated and decided on all aspects of communal work, including new projects. The assembly decided on such things as the establishment of small industries, the formation of a consumers' cooperative, the creation of workshops, and even the soliciting of individual loans from the *Agrarian Development Bank*. Needless to say, the assembly also handled all actions concerning the plunder of community lands.

A serious problem which the program had to face was the terrible reluctance on the part of the Indians to participate in the discussions and debates. It was necessary to stimulate those present constantly to overcome their inhibitions and to participate actively. In the beginning, someone from the program (usually myself), had to direct questions at individuals to get them to express their opinions on the matter being discussed by the assembly. This was difficult enough with the men, but it led to desperate contortions with the women, who shut themselves off and were very hard to get through to, perhaps because of the prevailing attitude that "the man is the head and it is the head that talks." Slowly, this resistance has weakened over the last few years, until today there is active participation in the assemblies, which has enabled us to begin turning complete control over to the local leaders.

Teamwork: the Internal Organization of the Program and its Relations with the Community

When the program began, we all gave ourselves completely to the work, not only offering suggestions but participating in the actual physical labor as well. In the construction of the school, the program personnel assisted the Indians in the preparation of mud, the making of adobe, and the carrying of rocks. By sharing in the manual labor, we were able not only to encourage the peasants but also to develop a sense of solidarity with them, as nothing unites individuals better than common work and hardships. In this way we were able to demonstrate to the community that, although we were Mestizos, we really were interested in helping them.

From the beginning, we viewed our work as cooperative and integrated. Although each member of the program had his own specialty, he did not devote himself exclusively to this area of concern, but rather felt responsible for the success of the program as a whole. The common obligation of the personnel was to carry forward the concrete work of the program, without stopping to think about to whom a project "belonged" or personal glory. We gave this goal the title of "the impersonality of the action," meaning that the success of the work as a whole was more important than the success of the concrete projects directed by various personnel, for only in this broader context could the achievements of the program be evaluated. In accord with this philosophy, individual projects were customarily discussed among the entire staff of the program prior to their initiation.

A group composed of individuals with different specialties and different personalities cannot coordinate its activities well from the outset, but must try to develop systems of coordination and integration as it operates. In the early stages of our program, there was some friction and resentment among the personnel which stood in the way of the solidarity needed to carry out our philosophy. A mechanism was needed to promote greater understanding among the members of the program. For this purpose, we established what we called "drainage sessions," which were monthly round-table meetings involving the entire staff. All personnel were on equal footing at these sessions, including the director of the program, and there was complete freedom of expression. These meetings provided individuals with the opportunity to air grievances and resentments, discuss their points of view on actions which they considered unjustified or arbitrary, and offer explanations of their own actions and beliefs in reply to comments made by others. The opportunity to give vent to tensions by frankly discussing personal differences led to an atmosphere of greater solidarity and friendship among the personnel. At first a certain reticence had to be overcome, especially when discussions concerned the director of the program, but as the meetings continued, the staff became accustomed to speaking freely and sincerely expressing their feelings and opinions. The initiation of these sessions was extremely effective in achieving the solidarity and mutual commitment we had hoped for in the program.

We had planned to have team meetings every two weeks to discuss the ongoing work, but during the early stages of the program we found it necessary to hold weekly meetings. The fact that we were all living and eating together gave us the chance to have continuous discussion of the program and its problems, and to develop a real sense of the group, so that in actuality the formal meetings served to make official our decisions and to clarify the aims of the projects and the steps to be taken in initiating them.

Meetings with the governing board and the community assembly were coordinated in advance with the personero. Together, the director of the program and the personero would plan the agendas for these meetings, and, according to the topics to be discussed, would decide which member of the program should attend the board meeting. The entire staff of field personnel attended the general assemblies, participating according to their specialties and the topics being discussed. The assemblies did not necessarily follow the prepared agendas, since the members of the community were free to introduce new topics of discussion at any time.

At first these assemblies were very confused and complicated, as the men constantly vacillated between supporting and rejecting motions, many times reversing their decisions after having approved a proposal. This was due in part to the reticence of the women, making it difficult for the men to know their thoughts on a topic. As we explained earlier, we had come to understand the role of the woman as being, in effect, the "power behind the throne." We therefore developed a new strategy taking this fact into account: proposals discussed at an assembly were not to be voted on immediately, but would be tabled until the next assembly. This greatly expedited matters, since the men had time to confer with their women before having to vote at the next meeting.

We also observed that many of the actions carried out by the community suffered a collapse after some time, that is, were abandoned by the community, which seemed to lose interest in them. In these cases we have learned that the best procedure on our part is not to insist upon the activity in question, but to ignore the matter and assume an attitude of indifference toward it. This has produced good results, for the matter left unattended begins to intrigue the people, leading to a renewal of interest in the project.

These experiences, together with the failure of the fireplace remodeling project, led us to adopt the following as a basic operating principle: "Wait for the people to suggest or demand an action." It is true that we introduced suggestions informally in casual conversations to indirectly bring about the initiation of projects. We would use every opportunity—casual conversations, rest periods, family festivities—to keep our ideas "in the air," until finally the Indians would make them their own. We found that in this way the Indians carried forward the projects with greater conviction, feeling that the ideas had originated in the community and had not been imposed by outsiders. Thus the stimuli which we provided raised the general level of expectation of the Indians, who eventually took some initiatives, in response to which the program was able to organize work projects. Examples of such projects include the carpentry workshop, the consumers' cooperative in Kuyo Chico, and a production cooperative in Kuyo Grande.

We have already mentioned that the supply of salt and kerosene was in the hands of the Mestizo businessmen in Pisaq, who, given the necessity of these articles, were able to impose whatever prices and system of sales they desired on the Indians. As we indicated earlier, not only were exorbitant prices charged, but the Mestizos established a system whereby these items could not be purchased with money, but only in exchange for such articles as cheese, eggs, and milk, which were appraised according to the caprice of the businessmen.

This problem was raised by the peasants at one of the assemblies, and they asked if the program could do something about it. One person asked specifically that we take charge of bringing the salt and kerosene to the community, where we could sell them to the peasants at fair prices. We explained that our program could not take on business activities, but suggested that they might do it themselves, by investing in shares of a community fund set up for this purpose. We pointed out that these articles could be bought at cost and then sold at a profit in the community, and also at moderate prices in other communities. The investors would be able to purchase these articles with money and at much lower prices. Finally, we suggested that each family head who wanted to invest in the business could buy one or more shares at ten soles each (about 37 cents). The community accepted this proposal, and immediately there were fifty shareholders. At a later assembly, the cooperative was organized so that each investor would take a turn at handling the sales, in regular rotation. The first acquisition of kerosene was made while the program initiated procedures with the *Caja de Depósitos y Consignaciones* (the agency charged with tax collection) to grant the community a license for selling salt.

As a result of the operations of this cooperative, the system of selling salt and kerosene in Pisaq has been changed, and these articles are now sold as they are everywhere else, in exchange for money. The community now has access to such foods as milk, eggs, and cheese, which are included in the regular diets of many families. The cooperative has stopped functioning for the present, by agreement of the community, in order to devote full capital and efforts to a final attempt to regain the lands under litigation.

Approximately twenty-five years ago, the community was

involved in a suit in Kuyo Grande with one of the neighboring haciendas, with several members of the community bearing the costs of the litigation. The community did not reimburse these individuals, and so they took over eight topos of land belonging to the community. Later, some other members of the community were named school deputies by the provincial office of education. These people, counseled by teachers in the school, reclaimed the land in order to cede it to the Ministry of Education through a public document witnessed by the notary of Calca. Those in possession of the land refused to relinquish it to the teachers, claiming that, since these were community lands, no individual members of the community had the right to dispose of them. These people, together with their families and friends, opposed the school deputies and their families and friends, thus dividing the community into two warring bands. The tension between these two groups had built up to such an extent that open fighting was about to break out.

At this point, the personero asked us to intervene in the matter. First we talked privately with the two parties involved. After hearing their positions, we explained to them what we took to be the legal status of their claims. Afterwards we had the governing board call a community assembly, at which we explained that these were community-owned lands and, because they were owned by the community as a whole, the only authority which could cede them was the legal personero, with the approval of the assembly. Since the school deputies did not constitute a representative community authority, their donation was legally null and void. In addition, we expressed the opinion that those who had possessed the land during the last twenty-five years had been adequately repaid for their original outlay, through all the harvests they had obtained. Thus we proposed that they return the land to the community. After some discussion, they agreed to our proposal, but asked that they be allowed to harvest the crop currently planted on the land and that the repossessed land be used for the good of the community as a whole. The governing board established a production cooperative with this land, and the first crop planted was malt-ing barley. The profits gained through this cooperative went toward establishing a similar one in Kuyo Grande.

There are many additional examples of actions which arose in response to initiatives of the community, including the introduction of fruit trees, the raising of fowl, and the organization of family gardens. We shall not discuss these projects in detail here.

4

The Results of the Program

The Impact of the Program outside Kuyo Chico

Many of the actions carried out in Kuyo Chico were seen by the Indians of the surrounding communities as nothing short of sensational, particularly those actions concerning relations with the Mestizo world. Our spectacular successes soon produced similar projects in other communities, so that many of the changes we introduced became widespread in the area.

For example, the Indians of Kuyo Chico were the first to refuse to attend the faenas and unpaid work projects organized by the Mestizos in Pisaq. In conversing with the personero of Viacha some time later, we asked him why the members of his community had stopped going to the faenas. He recalled that one evening, after the lieutenant governor had arrived to announce a faena, they had all gathered to discuss the problem. All had agreed that Kuyo Chico had been able to resist the Mestizos because of the protection of our program, the proof being that the Kuyos had refused to attend and nothing had happened to them. They considered doing the same, but were afraid. One of the Indians had then proposed that they send a commission to us, to ask if they too might stop attending. A meeting with one of our personnel confirmed what they had already heard from the Indians of Kuyo Chico: that this type of work was prohibited by law and that no one could force them to do it. They then decided not to participate in the faenas any more, and when the agents from the town arrived, they refused to accompany them, telling them to see us if they had any complaints.

The communities of Kuyo Chico, Qotobamba, Mask'a, Kuyo Grande, Amphay, Viacha, and Amaru were the first to stop attending the faenas, and they were soon followed by many other communities, despite the threats of the Mestizo authorities. The Mestizos could not find sufficient grounds for continuing to pressure the Indians, whose defense we had assumed. This attitude spread beyond the borders of the district, reaching some communities in the province of Paucartambo. In T'oqra, for example, the Indians refused to attend a faena called by *Cooperación Popular* in Qolqepata. In this way the forced labor imposed on the Indians was ended.

It is undeniable that the spectacular successes of such projects as the building of the irrigation ditch, the remodeling of homes, the literacy campaign, the planting of trees, and the repair of the community road attracted the attention and interest of the Indians in other communities, who would often stop on their way through Kuyo Chico to talk with the peasants and the members of the program. The cabecillas and alcaldes of other communities started contacting the program, and we made efforts to establish more permanent relations with them. We started our work with the communities of Mask'a, Qotobamba, Kuyo Grande, and Amphay, and then slowly expanded our operations to include Amaru, Chawaytirí, Sakaka, Qamawara, Qotataki, and Viacha, which together with Kuyo Chico comprise eleven communities with a population of 6,564. Given our limitations of staff and resources, we did not want to expand the program beyond these communities, but, even so, we maintained less frequent relations and moderate influence with the more distant communities of Pillawara, Siusa, Paru Paru, Oqoruro, Qoyaqosqo, Qoyaruna, Killway, Uchumuka, T'irakancha, Lamay, Taray, and Pisaq itself, which together have a population of 12,139. Thus we had started working with 350 people in Kuyo Chico, and gradually expanded our operations until today 18,703 people have felt the influence of the program.

It is obvious that only the communities in the first group, those immediately surrounding Kuyo Chico, could receive careful attention from the program. Kuyo Grande was one of the first to ask for our assistance in finishing a school, for which we contributed materials and technical assistance. Later on, this first relation led to the organization of a governing board which united the traditional authorities with the newly elected ones. Sports activities were introduced, leading to the formation of teams and the construction of a regulation stadium. An agricultural cooperative was started, through which we introduced the use of agricultural loans from the Agrarian Development Bank. Other innovations included literacy centers, tile manufacture, a clothes-making workshop, a forestry program, and a health campaign.

Similar programs were executed in the other communities under our immediate influence, according to the existing conditions in each community. Actions were directed toward the improvement of roads, the remodeling of homes, the construction of reservoirs and irrigation ditches, laying claim to mines, the construction of ovens for firing clay, the construction of civic centers and sewing workshops, the improvement of schools, and health, forestry, and literacy campaigns.

We must make separate mention here of Amaru, since before coming to the program this community was tied to the Federation of Workers, which had organized a union. The peasants did not want us to know about this and did not mention it when we conferred with them. They were interested in the construction of a school, and we offered to help, given one condition: that they establish a governing board to organize the work. In addition to this, they wanted to obtain legal recognition for the community.

Several days later the cabecilla of Amaru came to talk to us. He said that several nights earlier some Mestizos had come to see them and proposed that the community organize a union, and that he had come to solicit our opinion in the matter. We did not let on that we knew the union had been in existence for several months, but told him that it seemed like a good idea to have the union, as it was important to organize the community. The subject did not come up again.

A governing board was established, and it decided to construct a social services center, which could house the school as well as a meeting room, workshops, dining hall, and medical post. We provided the necessary materials and had plans drawn up, which were given to the personnel working with the project. To date, a building of eight rooms has been completed and is in use. The ongoing contact which this project has required has been used to encourage the inauguration of a literacy program, work on an irrigation ditch, and participation in the construction of a hospital. All of this concentrated the interest of the people on the community, and they eventually abandoned the union, considering it a "waste of time."

The changes which occurred on the hacienda at Chawaytiri are of considerable interest. The program came to be involved because the Cuzco Federation of Workers had organized a union on this hacienda, with the aim of bringing the peasants to demand certain labor rights. The union demanded that the hacendado raise the pay and improve the living and working conditions of the *colonos*. They presented a dossier of grievances, which included a demand for the creation of a school, for which the hacendado refused to donate the required land. Both parties were passionate in their convictions, and soon violence resulted. The landowner had to leave the hacienda, and the union did not permit him to return for some time. This situation would have led to the intervention of the police, to the disadvantage of the peasants. The secretary of the union came to our office in Kuyo Chico and explained the situation, adding that they had obtained a raise in pay and some changes in the working conditions, but that the point of conflict was the donation of land for the school. We offered to mediate in the dispute, but had great difficulty in obtaining an interview with the hacendado, who considered our program a "hotbed of communists" and a "center for the subversion of the Indians." An occasion had to be created for us to speak with the hacendado.

The Mestizos of Cuzco celebrate the festival of All Saints in November with parties and the baptism of bread dolls. The program personnel, together with the Peace Corps workers who were associated with us at that time, decided to hold a party and baptize a doll. The doctor, who had good relations (including family ties) with the hacendado, invited him to the party, which he attended reluctantly in the company of a police captain of Calca. During the party, we explained our work to them, and in the end they were convinced that we were not subversives or "communist agitators." We brought up the subject of the hacienda and offered to mediate in the dispute, promising to have the peasants allow him to return to his land, if he would agree to the donation of land for the construction of the school, whose operations we would be responsible for supervising. He said that it would be awkward for him to cede the land to the Ministry of Education, whereupon we replied that he could donate one hectare to the Ministry of Labor and Indian Affairs if he preferred, or else directly to the National Plan for Integration, which he agreed to do.

We notified the union of this agreement, and on a designated day agreed to by both parties, we assembled on the hacienda with the landowner, to select and mark off the land to be ceded. Some time later we drew up a rough draft of the agreement, and when the hacendado died a few months later, his widow signed the official document granting the land for the school, in accord with her husband's wishes. We helped Chawaytirí to construct a civic center which also housed the school, covering the costs of the building materials and providing technical assistance. Through this contact we established long-lasting relations with Chawaytirí, which had the character of mutual collaboration and thus paralleled the relations which Kuyo Chico had established with the other communities. An indication of this is the fact that Chawaytirí attended the intercommunity assembly of delegates from twenty-two communities, which met to organize the *Junta*

Intercommunal de Desarrollo Campesino (Board of Peasant Intercommunity Development).

Pisaq and the Mestizos

When the program began, the town of Pisaq had a depressing appearance—the old, worn look which comes from neglect. The buildings were either a mud color or showed the last vestiges of a whitewash once received to whiten them. Worn down roofs of tile or straw crowned the houses, whose thin windows had been blackened by smoke. The town had no water pipes, and only three houses had toilets—boxes placed above a canal. There was no electricity, and the homes were lit by candles or, in some cases, kerosene lamps.

Because of their disdain for the Indians, the Mestizos were startled to see what had been accomplished by the "uppity Indians of Kuyo Chico." They seemed to take the accomplishments of the Kuyos as a deliberate provocation. For example, the visible improvements in the homes were taken as signs of defiance and insult placed by the side of the road. The Mestizos made cutting remarks about us, such as "They are improving the Indian houses but will soon see that this is like giving pastry to pigs." "Now even the Indians want to live like people." "There is no merit in the improvement of the Indians' houses if you do it for them." And, "You want to make the Indians feel better and have gone so far as to paint their houses." Even the Mestizos who were sympathetic to the program could not suppress an expression of injured dignity when the subject of the Indian homes arose. They could not tolerate the idea that the Indians might live in better conditions than themselves, and their self-respect was injured to the point that they took the condition of their town to be humiliating. Not wanting to be left behind, the Mestizos were gripped by a fever which drove them to a big surge of rehabilitation, repairs, and new projects. Many of them, imitating Kuyo Chico, adorned their homes with cement stucco, metal windows and paint, and one house even boasted a metal door. Municipal ordinances were passed, and new efforts made to resume work on a hydroelectric plant, a park re-modeling program, and the installation of adequate drinking-water facilities.

We must confess that our program did not play any direct role in these accomplishments, but it is undeniable that concern for change surged as a consequence of the improvements made by a class the Mestizos considered inferior. The dominant class received a healthy emotional shock, which led them to wish to maintain their status. This impulse must have been strong indeed, for conditions were not as favorable for the Mestizo as they had been in the old days, when he could force the Indians to work for nothing or pay only a symbolic salary, the hurk'a. Through the actions of our program, forced and free labor had been abolished, and thus the Mestizos who were suddenly interested in public and private improvements had no alternative but to pay wages to the workers or do the work themselves. With great reluctance, they had to accept the situation.

The authorities were obliged to seek appropriations for the public works in order to be able to pay the wages, which still did not equal the minimum wage required by law. Adjustments had to be made in the private sector as well. The *Mozos*, who, following the typical Mestizos attitudes, considered working in the chacras beneath their dignity, have had to revert to working the land with their own hands, due to the lack of peons at their disposal. Today it is possible to find many Mozos working side by side with their peons.

Wages have also been introduced in some haciendas, and there is now at least one which pays the legal minimum wage.

The Impact of the Program in Kuyo Chico

One of the most important effects which the program had in Kuyo Chico was the hope and security it gave to the people, so that they were able to make efforts to regain the rights which had been taken from them by the Mestizos.

One of the most disheartening facts for the community had been the taking of half their lands, which occurred several years before we arrived, and was an action whose history went back to the time when Kuyo Chico was part of the province of Paucartambo. This had been very inconvenient for the Kuyos, who had to cover a considerable distance to get to the provincial capital to handle paperwork or register complaints, not to mention to give their services to the local authorities. Someone suggested to them that the community request to be annexed to the province of Calca, since the district of Pisaq in Calca was only a few kilometers away. One of the most powerful Mestizos in Pisaq offered to help them in their petition, on the agreement that, if it were successful, they would turn over to him the harvests of some of the community lands for a certain number of years.

The community was eventually annexed to Pisaq, and the Indians made their promised payments for many years. However, the hacendado then decided to take over these lands and others as well, claiming that they were part of his property. He took his case before the court in Calca, offering as evidence that fact that the Indians turned over the harvests of these lands to him. He also produced some forged land documents which had been constructed from papers on which the Indians had imprinted their fingerprints during their annexation appeal to the government, as well as the false testimony of some Mestizos who were willing to testify against the Indians. According to the Indians, the judge ruled against them, supporting the eviction, solely on the basis of the hacendado's testimony and some distorted versions of remarks which the Indians had made in another case, involving the charge of usurping land, which the hacendado had brought before the criminal court.

The eviction notice having been served, fires were set on the land, and the peasants driven off. The hacendado assigned colonos from the community of Qotobamba to work the land that had been vacated. Despite all this, twenty-four men had not yet lost hope, and signed a petition in 1952 demanding repeal of the eviction order and the return of the land. Their struggle was made long and difficult by the persecution they suffered at the hands of the hacendado, the arbitrary harassment of the authorities, including the imprisonment of some of the men, and the economic hardships involved in paying the court costs. These intimidations lessened, along with the general domination of the Mestizos after 1960, and the income from the tile industry enabled the Kuyos to renew their efforts.

In 1964, a judicial decision reversed the earlier eviction order and ordered the return of the lands to the Indians, ruling that the earlier decision had been based upon fraudulent evidence. The hacendado appealed the case to higher court. His defeat at the lower level suggested a new strategy to him: he would try to provoke a confrontation between the Indians of Kuyo Chico and those of Qotobamba, to whom he had turned over the use of the lands. Through a member of his family, he organized the "Board of Socio-Economic Development of Qotobamba," promising that the community could make even greater advances than those of Kuyo Chico. He then offered for sale the disputed lands which were in the possession of Qotobamba, trying in this way to provoke some conflict between the communities. The Kuyos went to the Indians of Qotobamba and explained that, as they had won their case in the lower court, so they would win in the higher court, and sooner or later the lands would be returned to them, in which case those who bought from the hacendado now would be dispossessed and lose their money. They also reminded them that the lands clearly belonged to Kuyo Chico. Qotobamba decided not to buy the lands, and the "Board of Socio-Economic Development" disappeared.

In December 1967, the superior court issued a verdict upholding the decision of the lower court. A new appeal brought the case to the Supreme Court, which ruled on June 16, 1968, that the land be returned to the Indians. The community took possession of the lands on October 17, concluding the litigation with the legal registration of the property on November 4, 1968.

If we add to this the fact that, during 1968, five topos of land which had belonged to the church were reincorporated into the community, through a donation by the archbishop of the diocese, we can see how many new prospects and possibilities have opened up for Kuyo Chico, given all that had been impossible for lack of land. Almost immediately after taking possession of the new lands, the governing board set aside a considerable portion of them for cooperative ventures. They also reserved a zone for the building of the new town, under a plan providing for running water, sewage disposal, electricity, a marketplace, and a civic center containing a school, meeting room, and church. The remainder of the land was distributed provisionally until the area would be measured and divided into equal plots, to be distributed among the community members by lot.

With enough land finally available, it is now possible to initiate a campaign to make agriculture more mechanized and systematic, as well as to consider the growing interest among the Indians in scientific agriculture. Because of this interest, they asked us in one of the final assemblies of the year to seek the appointment of an agricultural engineer to Kuyo Chico.

Since 1065, various families which had moved to the capital some time ago have come back to Kuyo Chico. During the final months of 1968, the personero received letters from other families which had moved to Lima, asking that they be allowed to return. The governing board resolved that during the parceling out of the land, some lots would be reserved for people who would reincorporate themselves into the community.

The difference between the average annual income of a family at the start of our program and the average income today is striking. Family income during this period has quintupled, rising from 1,800 soles to 9,000 soles. The standard of living has gone up, with eighteen families owning radios, fifteen sewing machines, and at least two or three bicycles. And despite the sizeable drain on the community from meeting court costs, there has been an increase in the acquisition of animals, the traditional form of saving for the peasants. The raising of animals has almost doubled, despite the fact that this type of investment requires land for pasture and the provision of forage. In addition, the amount of cultivable land has risen from 9.44 percent in 1959 to almost 50 percent today, due to the irrigation projects directed by the program. These projects not only opened up new lands for farming, but also secured the harvests of the lands already under cultivation. Finally, the availability of a controlled supply of water made possible a more efficient use of land which, together with an improved system of crop rotation, yielded two harvests per year where before there had only been one. It also made possible the introduction of new crops, such as onions, potatoes, and malting barley.

The prolonged litigation with the hacienda produced much anxiety in the community and focused its attention on the judicial proceedings. Upon finally acquiring the disputed lands, the situation was much more favorable for the introduction of modern agricultural techniques. Furthermore, the recovered lands are excellent for these purposes, being supplied with enough water for irrigation.

This state of awaiting the outcome of the litigation also resulted in the suspension of activities directed toward home improvement or the construction of new houses. Also there was the prospect of using energies and economic resources in the construction of a new town if the community acquired the lands belonging to the church. With the acquisition of the new lands, the Indians have become eager to start work on this project.

The impact of the literacy campaign should not be evaluated solely by the number of people who can read and write, although we can point to a 25 to 30 percent reduction in illiteracy and monolinguism. The chief importance of this action has been the changes effected in the attitudes of the community. The success of the adult educational program brought an increased confidence in the teachers and the program, which led to a much higher level of school attendance than ever before. As we indicated earlier, Kuyo Chico is the only community in the entire province of Calca to have eliminated the problem of school absenteeism. Particularly significant is the increased attendance of girls, indicating a change in the traditional attitudes concerning the importance of education for women. In addition, this campaign has raised the level of sociocultural participation of the community. Kuyo Chico students are now in high school, and many plan to attend the university or technical schools. Civic participation has increased with the ability to obtain voting cards. We can claim that Kuyo Chico is the first community in the area whose women have participated in national elections, and also that it has the greatest number of voters in the district, a fact which has given the community a sense of responsibility and security, and a clearer perception of the national life. Since the voting card is also proof of citizenship and is required for entering into various contractual arrangements, reading and writing are no longer merely considered signs of prestige but are viewed as offering the individual possibilities of expanding his sphere of activities.

A series of changes in the attitudes of the Indians toward certain traditional practices has also been brought about by the program, as they have realized the negative aspects of certain customs, such as the religious cargos. The understanding of the harmfulness of this practice enabled the community finally to abolish it.

Changes have also been effected in the nature of the Indian-Mestizo relations, which were of the master-servant type when we arrived. The Indian was constantly afraid, which greatly complicated his life. He was humble to the point of prostrating himself before the Mestizo. The existence of continual fear was accurately reflected in the behavior of the children, who fled terrified from the Mestizo, which contrasts greatly with the visible joviality of the children in Kuyo Chico today. The Indian would not look directly at the Mestizo when greeting him as *papay* ("my father"); if the Mestizo did not respond, he would repeat his greeting three or four times in the most humble way. Today if an Indian meets a Mestizo, he remains silent if he does not know him, or greets him as *señor* (the term commonly used among social equals in the Mestizo world) if he knows him, only when he is sure the Mestizo has seen him.

The Indian no longer tends to place himself in positions of

absolute inferiority and subordination. On one occasion, Justino, a young man of eighteen, was working in his garden near the road. A trustee of the church arrived on horseback, and after calling him said, "Monday you will come to work in my garden." Without becoming ruffled, Justino replied "Sir, I cannot come to work in your garden because I have to work in mine." This was considered insolent by the trustee, who got off his horse and approached Justino, saying, "I should knock all your teeth out so that you'll learn to answer your patrón without insolence." The youth, with the same tranquility, answered, "Sir, don't hit me, because if you do, I will hit you back. I'm from Kuyo Chico." The Mestizo, unaccustomed to such words and self-assurance, quickly realized that the prudent course of action would be to leave. He mounted his horse and rode away.

Other cases of various types indicate that the Indians of Kuyo Chico are gaining force in the management of their own destinies. Even so, more time will be needed before they can move with the boldness and self-confidence which will come with the full exercise of their rights. For too many years the community has lived under a system of domination and dependency which violated its members' most basic human rights. The dominant Mestizo group had taken on the image of the master, and the actions of the Indian depended on the will of the master.

When the program began, there was a substitution of images while a mechanism of dependence continued, this time with the program taking on a protective role in the relations of the Indians with the Mestizos. The program maintained this role of guardian for some time, as we considered it a mistake to suppose that the Indian could oppose the conditions existing in the area with no support. During the last two years, the cases in which the program has had to intervene have become very scarce, as the community board has assumed many of the roles which we had performed. It is no longer necessary for us to accompany the Indians when they go before the Mestizo authorities, as the personero or director of the board now does this. Step by step, the community has loosened the ties of dependency. Only when a complex situation arises do they now come to our office seeking advice and collaboration.

A New Type of Cholo?

In the sociocultural hierarchy of Peru, the Cholo has been identified as the type between the Indian and the Mestizo, having a low social status but a higher one than the Indian. He is a product of disorderly transculturation, as is indicated by his aggressiveness and emotional instability (switching from the norms of one culture to those of the other), his self-identification at variance with his true extraction, and his scorn for the Indian. He is a being whose aggressiveness is a result of an uprooting from his origins and the pressures from the higher strata which vigorously impede his progress up the social ladder. It is possible that a great deal of these characteristics result from the more or less violent transplanting of the individual from the community to the urban or semi-urban Mestizo centers, where he experiences much anxiety and difficulty in trying to find a way to survive.

It would seem that in Kuyo Chico, where change has occurred gradually, systematically, and within one society, the individual who, because of the process of transculturation he has undergone, could be considered a Cholo, might be a new kind of Cholo, with characteristics different from those of the traditional Cholo. He is a Cholo without prejudice toward the Indian—in fact, with a pride in identifying with the Indian—and consequently he does not feel the need to violently erase the past which characterizes the traditional Cholo. In Kuyo Chico he does not have a higher social position than the Indian, but shares the same standing with him, although like the traditional Cholo he dresses differently, reads and writes Spanish, and tends to seek involvement in activities beyond exclusive devotion to agriculture. He is highly stable and secure, in contrast to the unpredictable and emotional traditional Cholo. We conclude that in Kuyo Chico a new type of Cholo is emerging, one who has undergone cultural change while maintaining a high degree of stability within his group.

Costs and Accomplishments

In any work of directed social change, be it called "applied anthropology" or "community development," the material results are evidence of the less tangible impact of the program upon the consciousness of individuals. These results are and must be expressions of the changes which have taken place in the system of ideas which orders the life of the society. Without this they would be meaningless intrusions; a building, a road, a school, are only important if the people see them as functional in their culture. We also feel that the tangible results of a program should not be considered investments, but rather the results of an applied investment. In the case of Kuyo Chico, the investment was the salaries of the field personnel, the wages of the laborers hired, and the costs of the building materials used in the program's projects. The accomplishments of the program are the results of the application of this investment, and can be translated into material value.

Our records give us the following figures on costs in dollars and physical value of the investments made.

COSTS

	Salaries	Wages	Other Expenses
1959	$ 5,035	$ 83	$ 2,930
1960	5,381	131	1,778
1961	6,682	1,746	2,995
1962	8,123	2,413	2,593
1963	11,785	1,936	4,483
1964	17,492	550	8,067
1965	24,052		13,066
1966	23,744		11,617
1967	21,426	313	9,992
	$123,720	$7,172	$57,521

Grant Total $188,413

ESTIMATED PHYSICAL VALUE OF INVESTMENTS
IN KUYO CHICO AREA

1.	Irrigation channel, 5 kms, for Kuyo Chico	$141,791
2.	Irrigation channel, 3 kms, for Amaru	9,328
3.	Irrigation channel, 2 kms, for Mask'a	7,462
4.	Civic center in Chawaytirí, 2 rooms	10,448
5.	Civic center in Amaru, 7 rooms	22,388
6.	Communal housing in Kuyo Chico, 2 apartments	2,985
7.	Communal kiln for tiles in Kuyo Chico	373
8.	Communal kiln for tiles in Qotobamba	373
9.	Communal kiln for tiles in Kuyo Grande	373
10.	Communal kiln for tiles in Amphay	299
11.	Communal kiln for tiles in Amaru	373
12.	Communal oven for bread baking in Kuyo Chico	373
13.	Regulation-size sports field in Kuyo Grande	2,239
14.	Finishing of school in Kuyo Chico	1,045
15.	Renovation of chapel in Sakaka	373
16.	Finishing of school in Warkhi	746
17.	Remodeling of 25 houses in Kuyo Chico and Mask'a	23,321
18.	Demonstration house in Amaru	187
19.	Installation of water (piping)	299
20.	Sanitary protection of 10 springs in Kuyo Chico, Mask'a, and Qotobamba	299
21.	10 latrines in Kuyo Chico, Kuyo Grande, and Qamawara	93
22.	Wall-size blackboard in Sakaka	15
23.	Staking claim for gypsum mine in Amphay	560
24.	Dirt road Kuyo Chico-Viacha, 3 kms	149
25.	Repair of road Amphay-Qotataki-Qamawara	149
26.	Building for Kuyo Chico campesino hospital & connecting road	55,970
27.	30,000 eucalyptus trees for Kuyo Chico, Kuyo Grande, Amaru, Mask'a, Qotobamba, and Paru-Paru	223,881
28.	Installation of electric light in Kuyo Chico	5,597
29.	Expansion of school in Kuyo Chico	2,239
30.	2 latrines in San Salvador	112
31.	Installation of water pump in Vilcabamba	93
32.	Reservoir in Kay-Kay	157
33.	100 fruit trees (peach and plum) in Kuyo Chico	373
	Total Physical Value of Improvements	$514,463

Note: On January 3, 1959, the Peruvian sol was quoted at 24.75 to the dollar. It fluctuated between this point and 28.75 during the rest of that year. The sol was stabilized at 26.80, where it remained until September of 1967, at which time it broke sharply, eventually stabilizing at 43.38. Since the 26.80 figure is close to correct throughout practically all of the period of the program, the dollar figures are set at that rate in the above table.

From the point of view of the community, there is an additional factor to be considered in calculating the growth of its economic resources: the acquisition of the church lands (5 acres) and the recovery of the lands from the hacienda (100 acres). The average price of land in the region is 6,000 soles ($224) per acre, so these acquisitions are valued at approximately $23,520. It might be objected that these are not new resources, but simply represent a redistribution of resources. However, we must emphasize the fact that if the lands had belonged to the Indians, it cannot be claimed that these lands were taken from the church and hacienda, given the illegality of their holdings. Thus it cannot be assumed that what the Indians gained was lost by the Mestizos. On the contrary, the bettering of the Indian has contributed to the general improvement of the area, the resultant benefits being shared by the Mestizos. The situation should not be regarded as a dispute between sectors, but as a search for new opportunities for both. Efforts to achieve goals, independently or in collaboration, will benefit one or both sectors without hurting either. It is not a case of taking from the "haves" and giving to the "have-nots," but of achieving the general improvement of the region. In many cases the progress made by one sector serves to stimulate the other. Such was the case with the home improvement program of the Indians in Kuyo Chico, which induced the Mestizos to improve the conditions in the district capital.

5

The Evidence from the Surveys

William F. Whyte

How can the results of a program of applied anthropology be evaluated? We can express the value of physical improvements in economic terms, as has Núñez del Prado, and we can also note the concrete evidence of changes in political participation, demonstrated in the registration of voters. These data are certainly important, but they do not tell the whole story.

The applied anthropologist wishes to have some positive impact upon the human spirit. The researcher can present his impression of the impact of his program in this regard, but can such changes be measured?

This is the task we set ourselves in the Study of Change in Peruvian Communities, a research program carried out jointly by the Instituto de Estudios Peruanos and Cornell University. Codirectors of this program were José Matos Mar for IEP and Lawrence K. Williams and the author for Cornell. Under our general direction, from February to October of 1964, students and professors of five Peruvian universities applied surveys in twenty-six villages in five areas of Peru.

It should be emphasized that the Kuyo Chico Program and the Study of Change in Peruvian Communities, which was begun five years after the first intervention in Kuyo Chico, were completely independent of each other. The author of this chapter has at no time had any responsibility for the applied anthropology program. While our survey team had the invaluable aid of Dr. Núñez del Prado in securing acceptance of our surveys in the Sacred Valley, we sought insofar as possible to maintain an identity separate from the applied anthropology program so as to assure the independence of a study which involved in part an evaluation of that program.

The 1964 survey in the Pisaq district was carried out by anthropology students at the University of Cuzco, under the direction of Núñez del Prado, with Hernán Castillo acting as consultant. Núñez del Prado prepared the Quechua translation of the questionnaire, which was used for all informants with inadequate knowledge of Spanish—most of those living outside of Pisaq. We sought to obtain a sample of at least 20 percent of the male and female adult population. For this purpose, we made a random selection of at least one of every five households and then attempted to give the survey to all of the adults living in each of the homes selected. For small communities, where 20 percent would have yielded too small a number of responses for statistical analysis, we increased the sample size. For example, in Kuyo Chico the sample of forty-nine represents approximately 40 percent of the adults then living in the community. We sought to obtain from each respondent his opinions of himself and of the people around him, his attitudes toward his community, and his attitudes toward his government, at the local, district, and national levels.

In order to measure the impact of the applied anthropology project, the ideal would have been to have a base-line study at the time of the beginning of intervention and then a restudy some years later. Since we cannot survey people retroactively, can we use the data from the 1964 study to determine what changes in Kuyo Chico might have occurred in response to intervention? In 1964 we also surveyed Pisaq, the district capital, a hacienda (Chawaytirí), and four Indian communities (Sakaka, Mask'a, Qotobamba, and Kuyo Grande).

While we have noted impacts of the program outside of

Kuyo Chico, the major intervention efforts were directed particularly at that community, and the Kuyos had much more
frequent opportunities for personal interaction with project
personnel than was the case for the other communities. We
may therefore assume that the effects of the program would
show up most strongly in Kuyo Chico. Thus, if the responses
in Kuyo Chico differ markedly from those in neighboring communities, we can attribute these differences at least in part
to the program.

In 1969 we carried out a resurvey, using many of the same
items contained in the 1964 questionnaire. Since we are not
now interested in the differences among the other Indian communities and since Sakaka and Kuyo Grande were not included in the 1969 studies, for both 1964 and 1969 we are
combining figures for Mask'a and Qotobamba, for comparison
with Kuyo Chico, Pisaq, and Chawaytirí. (In any case, for our
purposes, the 1964 figures for Sakaka and Kuyo Grande are
similar to those for Mask'a and Qotobamba.)

There are important advantages in being able to examine
the results of the two surveys. First, we made the 1964 study
when we had had very little experience with surveys in rural
Peru, while those who carried out the 1969 surveys had had
substantial experience and had fully demonstrated their capa-
bilities. Therefore, if in general terms the 1969 results confirm
the pattern found in 1964, we will have more confidence in
the validity of our conclusions. Also, certain changes in responses were to be expected, and the resurvey permits longi-
tudinal comparison.

In the best of circumstances, the questionnaire is not an
exact instrument. Therefore, we should not exaggerate the importance of the results on a single item, or the small differences among villages, which could have arisen through sam-
pling error. We should be concerned only with the *pattern* of
results—if a pattern appears. In this case, as we will see, the
data reflect a general pattern with impressive consistency.

To avoid burdening the reader with endless figures, in general we will limit ourselves to presenting in tables the 1969

responses, but always indicating how they resembled or differed from those obtained in 1964. Since there generally are differences by sex in the responses, for each community we show males and females separately.

The percentages in the tables to follow are all based upon the number of respondents per community as shown in table 1.

TABLE 1
NUMBER OF RESPONDENTS (1969)

	Males	Females
Pisaq	52	60
Chawaytirí	29	32
Mask'a-Qotobamba	51	51
Kuyo Chico	22	29

In some cases, to present the Cuzco results in a broader context, we compare them with the totals from the study of seventeen communities in the 1969 survey. Included in this study were three communities in the Mantaro Valley (central highlands), six from the Chancay Valley (central coast), and three from the Virú Valley (north coast).

While we cannot here point out all the events between 1964 and 1969 which might have changed Kuyo Chico responses in 1969, we should note two very important developments. During this period, Kuyo Chico finally won its case against the hacendado and thereby increased its cultivable lands by 50 percent. And two months prior to the 1969 survey, the government terminated the applied anthropology program and cut off all support in personnel or other resources. (See the Epilogue.) Even though during the first months it was impossible to foresee all the consequences of this abrupt termination, some negative reactions in Kuyo Chico could be anticipated. Would the reactions be shown in a loss of hope in their future, in a loss of confidence in themselves, or in a loss of confidence in the government? Or perhaps in all of these ways and in others as well? We will answer these questions in the analysis which follows.

Orientation toward the Community

Upon asking if they considered that their community was better than, worse than, or equal to other communities, we found the Kuyos less favorable than residents of Pisaq but more favorable than those in the hacienda and the other pair of communities.

To sum up the results, we struck a mean of the responses, coding "better than others" as 1, "like others" as 2, and "worse than others" as 3. In table 2, therefore, the lower the mean score, the more favorable the evaluation of the community.

TABLE 2

COMPARATIVE EVALUATION OF THE COMMUNITY

"How do you feel your village compares with other villages?"

	Kuyo Chico		Mask'a-Qotobamba		Chawaytirí		Pisaq	
	M	F	M	F	M	F	M	F
1964	1.87	1.36	2.29	2.03	1.68	1.70	1.44	1.41
1969	1.68	1.74	2.16	2.31	2.21	1.85	1.46	1.58

In comparison with 1964, the evaluation of the men in Kuyo Chico has risen while the evaluation of the women has dropped.

In perceptions of progress experienced in the community and also in their expectations for the future, the Kuyos answered in a much more favorable manner than the respondents in the other villages. We asked, "Think back on how you felt five years ago on the possibilities of economic progress for this village. Today do you feel more optimistic, the same, or more pessimistic?" Coding "more optimistic" as 1, "the same" as 2, and "more pessimistic" as 3, we have the result shown in table 3.

While the Kuyos became slightly more pessimistic over the five-year period, this negative shift was not nearly so marked as in the other communities.

When we asked respondents whether five years ago their village was better or worse off, whether five years in the fu-

TABLE 3
OPTIMISM/PESSIMISM REGARDING FUTURE COMMUNITY PROGRESS

	Kuyo Chico		Mask'a- Qotobamba		Chawaytirí		Pisaq	
	M	F	M	F	M	F	M	F
1964	1.05	1.18	1.17	1.79	1.23	1.75	1.17	1.33
1969	1.38	1.38	1.96	1.98	2.22	2.11	1.64	2.07

ture it would be better or worse off, and how in general they evaluated the rate of progress of their community, the Kuyos consistently gave responses that were markedly more favorable and optimistic than those obtained in the other communities.

In the questions regarding prevalence of conflict and degree of collaboration, Kuyo Chico offers evidence of a higher degree of solidarity than the rest of the villages, as shown in table 4.

TABLE 4
CONFLICT AND COLLABORATION

	Kuyo Chico		Mask'a- Qotobamba		Chawaytirí		Pisaq	
	M	F	M	F	M	F	M	F
	%		%		%		%	
Is there much con-flict among the people of this village?								
Much conflict	0	7	8	6	10	19	11	27
Some conflict	27	38	33	26	52	34	52	35
Hardly any or no conflict	73	52	59	61	34	37	29	17
NA	3	3	—	8	3	9	8	22
When it comes to working on a project for the benefit of the community, how well do the people cooperate?								
Much cooperation	59	59	49	49	48	47	21	33
Fair cooperation	36	28	33	26	17	22	38	23
Poor cooperation	4	7	14	18	28	9	33	23
No cooperation	—	3	2	4	7	12	6	12
NA	—	3	2	4	—	9	2	8

Compared with 1964, we find in both Kuyo Chico and Mask'a-Qotobamba a slight decrease in these indices of solidarity. In Chawaytirí, the decrease is so great as to give evidence of an internal crisis. Pisaq has hardly changed at all and remains in last place in solidarity.

Future Orientation

In three items concerning future orientation, we arrived at the following conclusions.

1. In general, the men are more future-oriented than the women.

2. The men of Kuyo Chico and of Pisaq surpass the other villages in future orientation. There is no significant difference between these two.

3. The women of Kuyo Chico surpass the women of the other villages by a wide margin.

4. In Kuyo Chico, future orientation appears to have increased during the five year period.

Orientation toward Work

In their belief that hard work promises significant rewards, Kuyo Chico surpasses the other villages. When they had to choose between an exacting employer who paid higher wages and a less exacting boss who paid lower wages, the Kuyos were more inclined than others to opt for the demanding work situation. We find the same result on the question of the utility of hard work for gaining a higher standard of living. On the question asking how other villagers would look upon an outstanding worker, we found a phenomenon on which we will comment after presenting table 5.

The most striking finding in this table is the high percentage of people who think that hard work would excite envy. Apparently the concern with envy is a very important theme in rural Peru; the answers from a total of seventeen villages included in the 1969 survey give us 63 percent of the men and 73 percent of the women who selected "they would envy

TABLE 5
ECONOMIC AND SOCIAL VALUE OF HARD WORK

	Kuyo Chico		Mask'a-Qotobamba		Chawaytirí		Pisaq	
	M	F	M	F	M	F	M	F
	%		%		%		%	
If you worked harder, do you believe you would have a higher standard of living?								
Yes	100	76	84	74	66	56	96	73
More or less	—	14	10	18	14	9	4	8
No	—	10	4	2	17	22	—	13
NA	—	—	2	6	3	12	—	5
If you worked very hard, what would other people in the community think of you?								
That you are a fool because it is not worth it	4	—	—	—	—	2	2	2
They would respect you more for it	14	10	16	4	14	9	25	7
They would envy you	59	86	80	94	76	81	67	87
Other answers and NA	23	—	4	2	10	9	6	5

you." (A comparison with 1964 results on this item is impossible because then we did not offer the envy alternative.)

Faith in People

Our earlier studies in Peru had revealed a low level of trust in others—an orientation which impedes development on any project requiring cooperation. Of the five items on this theme, three showed a small but not significant difference in favor of Kuyo Chico in the level of trust. The remaining two items shown in table 6 show an impressive difference in the same direction.

Putting these percentages in the context of the 1969 survey of eighteen villages, we find that only 20 percent of the men and 13 percent of the women answered that "one can trust most people," and only 13 percent of the men and 12 percent

TABLE 6
FAITH IN PEOPLE

	Kuyo Chico		Mask'a-Qotobamba		Chawaytirí		Pisaq	
	M	F	M	F	M	F	M	F
	%		%		%		%	
Some people say most people can be trusted. Others say you can't trust people. What do you say?								
Can trust people	50	38	43	35	31	12	15	17
Can't trust people	45	55	53	53	55	78	79	68
Other answers	4	7	2	12	14	9	6	15
Would you say that most people like to help others or like to watch out for themselves?								
Help others	41	41	29	24	21	9	19	17
Look out for selves	55	59	69	71	72	78	79	78
Other answers	4	—	2	2	7	12	—	4

of the women said that the majority of people "like to help others." Thus Kuyo Chico demonstrates a much higher level of trust than the average of all the other communities surveyed. Comparing the 1964 and 1969 results, we find a rise in the level of trust in Kuyo Chico.

Fatalism and Pessimism

On three abstract items regarding fate (for example, "Some were born to lead and others to follow"), we do not find systematic differences between Kuyo Chico and the other villages. On the other hand, in the questions that specifically refer to "poor people," "a poor man," or "the poor," we find much more optimism in Kuyo Chico, as shown in table 7.

Only for the first of the three items do we have an exact comparison with 1964. This comparison shows that the level of optimism regarding the lot of poor people has decreased in

TABLE 7
BELIEFS REGARDING THE LOT OF POOR PEOPLE

	Kuyo Chico		Mask'a-Qotobamba		Chawaytirí		Pisaq	
	M	F	M	F	M	F	M	F
	%		%		%		%	
The lot of poor people is getting worse.								
Agree	50	48	59	45	76	59	67	78
Partially agree	18	21	33	47	14	28	15	13
Disagree	32	28	8	8	3	6	17	7
NA	—	3	—	—	7	6	—	—
What possibilities does a poor man have to better his economic condition?								
Many	85	79	69	61	66	62	56	57
Some	15	21	28	28	31	22	38	32
None	—	—	4	10	3	12	6	10
NA	—	—	—	2	—	3	—	2
Some say the rich are getting richer and the poor are getting poorer.								
True	41	48	47	55	55	62	71	77
More or less true	32	17	33	26	24	12	10	5
False	27	34	18	18	21	22	19	17
NA	—	—	2	3	—	5	—	3

Pisaq, has increased somewhat in Chawaytirí and Mask'a-Qotobamba, and has increased greatly in Kuyo Chico. On these items, Kuyo Chico expresses much more optimism than the average of our seventeen communities.

Traditionalism-Modernity

In two items on this dimension, we find the men of Kuyo Chico surpassing the other villages in modern orientation, by a wide margin. In general, the women are more tradition-oriented than the men, and those of Kuyo Chico are no exception, as we see in table 8.

TABLE 8

TRADITIONALISM—MODERNITY

	Kuyo Chico		Mask'a-Qotobamba		Chawaytirí		Pisaq	
	M	F	M	F	M	F	M	F
	%		%		%		%	
We should live like our ancestors in order to have a better life.								
Agree	46	59	51	61	86	75	52	58
Partially agree	—	14	24	22	10	19	10	15
Disagree	50	24	26	14	3	3	37	22
NA	4	3	—	4	—	3	—	5
It is difficult for a person to adopt new customs.								
Agree	36	69	55	63	69	56	52	65
Partially agree	14	17	18	11	17	19	14	12
Disagree	50	14	28	22	14	16	35	22
NA	—	—	—	2	—	9	—	—

There has been no notable change between 1964 and 1969 in responses to the first of these two items. (The second was not included in the 1964 survey.) In comparison with the other Cuzco villages, the men of Kuyo Chico are less tradition-oriented, while the women do not differ from the average.

Civic Orientation

The first requirement for political participation is the possession of the voting card. In this respect, Pisaq is naturally in first place, but Kuyo Chico is in second place with 23 percent of the men and 14 percent of the women qualified to vote. The figures for Mask'a-Qotobamba are 14 percent and 2 percent and for Chawaytirí 10 percent and 0 percent. We do not find significant changes in these proportions between 1964 and 1969. (There was no national election between these years.)

Of special interest is the nearly universal desire to obtain a voting card, as we see in table 9.

TABLE 9
DESIRE TO BECOME A REGISTERED VOTER

	Kuyo Chico		Mask'a-Qotobamba		Chawaytirí		Pisaq	
	M	F	M	F	M	F	M	F
	%		%		%		%	
Do you wish to obtain a voting card in the future?								
"Yes" among those not voters now	88	80	90	80	87	69	88	66

When we put these findings in the context of the informants of the seventeen villages, we find that the average "yes" response among those not having voting cards is 82 percent for men and 65 percent for women. Although this desire is already widespread, we find that the men in all of our Cuzco villages and the women of Kuyo Chico and Mask'a-Qotobamba show a markedly greater desire for the voting card than those surveyed elsewhere.

Has this desire increased between 1964 and 1969? Unfortunately we cannot make an exact comparison, because in 1964 we asked "Are you thinking of obtaining a voting card in the future?" "Thinking of" (*pensar*) suggests having a more or less definite idea, while "wish to" (*querer*) can indicate a simple desire without any consideration of the possibilities of realization. Given the difference in the two items, the

TABLE 10
THE IDEA OF OBTAINING THE VOTING CARD (1964)

	Kuyo Chico		Mask'a-Qotobamba		Chawaytirí		Pisaq	
	M	F	M	F	M	F	M	F
	%		%		%		%	
Are you thinking of obtaining a voting card in the future?								
"Yes" among those not voters now	70	30	28	7	36	0	50	38

marked rise in the "yes" answers throughout the seventeen villages was to be expected. Even so, let us look at the 1964 figures to see if we can discover any trend.

In 1964 Kuyo Chico had an enormous advantage over the other villages for males, and the females were a close second to those of Pisaq. In the 1969 item, we see that the other villages have gained parity with Kuyo Chico. Imperfect as it is, this 1964–69 comparison suggests that the civic activism of Kuyo Chico may have had a contagious impact.

We also asked one informational question: "Do you remember the name of the President of the Republic?" Table 11 shows the percentages of correct response.

TABLE 11
IDENTIFICATION OF THE PRESIDENT

	Kuyo Chico		Mask'a-Qotobamba		Chawaytiri		Pisaq	
	M	F	M	F	M	F	M	F
	%		%		%		%	
Correct identification of the President	54	7	29	0	17	0	50	13

In the seventeen villages, we obtained an average of 68 percent correct answers for men and 32 percent for women. As we had expected, all of our Cuzco villages are below the average in political awareness. Even so, it is impressive to find the men of Kuyo Chico surpassing the Mestizo town of Pisaq, though only by an insignificant 4 percent difference. Without a development project, we would expect to find an Indian community in Cuzco well below a Mestizo town in level of political awareness.

We sought to measure potential activism in political and civic affairs with four items. The traditional peasant is likely to have little faith in his ability to resolve the problems of his village. If the national or municipal government proposes to do something which he considers unjust, he feels incapable of offering any resistance, and he has no idea what tactics might be effective. When asked what he would do if he were

president of the country, the idea seems so incomprehensible
to him that it is almost impossible for him to respond. As we
see in table 12, the responses of Kuyo Chico show none of
these attitudes.

As table 12 shows, the men of Kuyo Chico are far ahead
of the men of the other Cuzco villages in their activist orientation. They are also well above the average seventeen communities in our broader study, and the Kuyo Chico women are
somewhat above the women's average for the total study.

TABLE 12
POTENTIAL ACTIVISM

	Kuyo Chico		Mask'a-Qotobamba		Chawaytirí		Pisaq	
	M %	F	M %	F	M %	F	M %	F
What chance do you and others like you have to solve the problems of this community?								
Very good	55	57	53	55	35	25	35	25
Fair	36	24	31	26	24	25	39	38
No chance	4	14	14	14	35	34	27	23
NA	4	3	2	6	7	16	—	14
Suppose the government wanted to do something bad or unjust. What could you do to prevent it?								
Able to respond	73	21	47	37	28	9	54	33
Suppose the municipal council wanted to do something bad or unjust, what could you do to prevent it?								
Able to respond	100	31	74	33	41	19	71	47
If you were President of the Republic, what would you do?								
Able to respond	100	59	77	37	45	31	85	62

132

In 1964, in an effort to measure only confidence in the courts, we asked the following question:

Some say that in the courts of Peru the decisions of the judges are based, above all, on the law and on the acts committed. Others say what counts more is "pull" and money. Which of these opinions comes closest to your own?

In the twenty-six-village study of 1964, we obtained an impressive result: Kuyo Chico was the only one which cast more votes for "the law and (on) the acts committed." In 1969 we used the same idea in simplified form, also with surprising results.

In 1964 the Kuyos were hoping to win their case against the hacendado, but the victory had not yet been won. In 1969 Kuyo Chico was already enjoying the fruits of its judicial victory, which might have been expected to produce an even more favorable evaluation of the system of justice. Instead of this, we find an almost universal negative reaction, one markedly more negative than in the other communities. This change must remain a mystery until we have the opportunity to carry out further anthropological studies in the area.

Relations between the Mestizos and Indians

In 1964 but not in 1969 we asked a series of questions on relations between Mestizos and Indians. Let us look at some of these 1964 results.

Is the Indian inherently inferior to the Mestizos? To the statement that Indians were born to serve and obey Mestizos, Kuyo Chico expressed the strongest disagreement, with the exception of Pisaq. Although in Pisaq many act as though the statement were true, it seems improbable that those individuals with some degree of education or who have otherwise been exposed to the democratic ideology would be inclined to express openly their belief in the Indian's inborn inferiority.

To what degree is there a relationship between the inferior

How do we compare the level of activism of 1964 with that of 1969? In 1964 we used only the first item, that of the possibility of resolving the problems of the community. The comparison on this item reveals a marked loss of confidence in Chawaytirí and an insignificant decrease in the other villages.

We measured the confidence of respondents in their national government with the two items shown in table 13.

TABLE 13
CONFIDENCE IN THE NATIONAL GOVERNMENT

	Kuyo Chico		Mask'a-Qotobamba		Chawaytirí		Pisaq	
	M	F	M	F	M	F	M	F
	%		%		%		%	
In general, would you say the activities of the government help to improve the conditions of the country?								
Yes	73	48	75	41	65	16	77	53
More or less	14	28	10	35	21	25	15	10
No	14	17	14	8	3	28	4	17
NA	—	7	2	16	6	31	4	20
Some say the government takes no interest in the problems of the people.								
Agree	36	24	29	33	31	31	27	23
Partially agree	27	41	20	39	17	31	17	17
Disagree	18	28	45	18	35	6	54	40
NA	18	6	6	10	17	31	2	20

We see that on these two items Pisaq expresses more confidence in the national government than the other communities. On the first item, the men of Kuyo Chico give responses similar to those of Mask'a-Qotobamba and Chawaytirí. The women show more confidence than those of Chawaytirí but not more than the women of Mask'a-Qotobamba. On the second item, the men of Kuyo Chico are more negative than the other male villagers, while the women are more favorable than those of Mask'a-Qotobamba and Chawaytirí.

For these items, the most interesting comparison is between the 1964 and 1969 figures. In 1964 Kuyo Chico expressed much more confidence than the other Cuzco communities in the national government; this level of confidence fell markedly in the five-year period. For example, in 1964 55 percent of the men and 64 percent of the women rejected the statement that "the government takes no interest in the problems of the people," and in 1969 this rate of rejection had dropped to 18 percent and 28 percent respectively. On this particular item, Kuyo Chico demonstrated more negativism toward the government than the average of the seventeen communities in our larger study.

In their attitude toward the municipality (of which they are a small part), in 1964 Kuyo Chico showed slightly more negativism than the other communities. In 1969 the reactions in Kuyo Chico are much more negative, with 96 percent of the men and 66 percent of the women saying that the municipality "does not help." In Mask'a-Qotobamba and Chawaytirí we also observe a decrease in confidence but not in such a drastic manner.

In 1964 Kuyo Chico almost unanimously expressed confidence in the effectiveness of its local community government, being far more favorable on this item than the other Indian communities. By 1969 this confidence had dropped slightly, but still almost three-fourths of the respondents of both sexes agreed that their community council "greatly improves conditions"—a vote far superior to that found in Mask'a-Qotobamba. (The item was not applied in the other two communities, which do not have this form of local government.)

How much confidence do the informants have in the possibilities of getting justice in the courts and in their relations with the police? On the first item in table 14 we see that Kuyo Chico surpasses the other villages in confidence in the courts. In relation to the police, the women of Kuyo Chico, surprisingly, express more confidence than the men. The men rank second to Mask'a-Qotobamba in this regard. Note the high proportion of men in Pisaq and of respondents of both sexes

in Chawaytirí who see no possibility of freeing from the police.

Due to changes in the form of the questions, it i to make an exact comparison between the 196 results. Even so, we can say that in 1964 Pisaq in the expression of this type of confidence, w Kuyo Chico showed a marked advantage over Pis

TABLE 14
REACTIONS TO THE COURTS AND THE PO

	Kuyo Chico		Mask'a-Qotobamba		Chawa
	M	F	M	F	M
	%		%		%
If you got involved in a court case, do you believe you would get a just decision?					
Yes	73	38	53	29	48
No	23	52	43	63	52
Other responses	4	10	4	8	—
Suppose you were accused before the police of slander. What chances would you have of going free?					
Good	27	55	43	24	38
Fair	54	14	37	55	24
Poor	4	14	8	16	3
None	9	17	8	12	34
Other responses	3	—	4	14	—

The two items in table 14 are related to two di confidence in institutions and the informant's sonal efficacy. That is, the informant may hav dence in an institution yet believe he has the abi ulate it for his own ends, and for this reason he optimistic manner.

position of the Indian and his lack of formal education? In all of the communities, the great majority stated that if the Indian had the same level of education as the Mestizo, he would be just as capable of performing well in any occupation. Kuyo Chico came closest to unanimity on this point.

We asked our informants if they thought relations between Indians and Mestizos were good, fair, or poor in their area. Kuyo Chico gave a more negative evaluation of the quality of these relations than any other community, with Pisaq in second place. We are confronted here with an apparent paradox: in the hacienda and the four Indian communities where fewer improvements had taken place in the economic, social, and political conditions, we find impressive testimony regarding the good quality of Indian-Mestizo relations, while in Kuyo Chico, where the most spectacular improvements have taken place, we find much more negative evaluations.

Apparently this illustrates what seems to be a common phenomenon during the course of a social change in which a subordinated people are in the process of attaining a level of equality with the dominant group. Although we do not have measurements to substantiate this conclusion, our understanding of race relations in the United States suggests that the Afro-Americans would have expressed greater satisfaction fifteen or twenty years ago with the quality of race relations than they do now, in spite of the great improvements gained in civil rights and other aspects of life.

We interpret these two situations to suggest that, as long as a group remains firmly subjugated and there is no perceived possibility of improving their condition, there will be a tendency for them to adapt themselves to what appears to be inevitable, to the point that they may even be able to find some positive aspects in their situation. To the extent that the former social equilibrium is disturbed and a subordinated group starts to improve its position, its members experience a sharpening of conflict with the superior group and become less inclined to consider their position of inferiority as inevitable. Therefore, a greater perception of conflict can be expected on the part of a subordinated group which is moving upward than in a group which remains in a static condition of domination.

To the extent that the previously subordinated group is gradually accepted on a more equal basis by those who had held positions of authority, we can expect that a new state of equilibrium will be reached and that the perceptions of the quality of the relations will again be more favorable. We can only verify this hypothesis indirectly. Since it was the applied anthropology program which brought about the change in the distribution of power, in 1964 we had predicted negative reactions among the respondents of Pisaq and a change toward a more favorable evaluation in 1969, which is, in fact, what we found.

We asked, "What effect do you think the applied anthropology program has had in this area?" We offered five alternatives ranging from "very favorable" to "very unfavorable." When we omit the informants who did not answer or who said "neither favorable nor unfavorable," we find that in Pisaq the percentage of favorable answers had risen between 1964 and 1969 from 38 to 63.

In Kuyo Chico, in 1969 as in 1964, there was not a single negative vote, but the level of enthusiasm was a little lower: in 1964 96 percent of the respondents answered "very favorable" as against 76 percent in 1969. In Mask'a-Qotobamba and in Chawaytirí there was a slight decrease in the "very favorable" category, and for the first time a few negative voices were heard, but the responses remained overwhelmingly favorable.

Changes in Economic Resources

In order to evaluate changes in economic conditions, we selected artefacts generally associated with the process of modernization, and we asked the informants in both years if they owned these articles. Since these are mainly objects owned by the family, in table 15 we do not separate respondents by sex.

TABLE 15

POSSESSION OF MODERN ARTEFACTS IN 1964 AND 1969

	Kuyo Chico		Mask'a-Qotobamba		Chawaytirí		Pisaq	
	'64	'69	'64	'69	'64	'69	'64	'69
	%		%		%		%	
Radio	10	26	0	14	0	2	33	45
Sewing machine	12	24	4	4	0	7	40	45
Kerosene stove or primus stove	16	24	0	11	0	5	17	39
Watch or clock	10	14	0	4	0	0	29	33
Bicycle	4	8	0	2	0	0	9	18
Truck, tractor, or automobile	0	2	0	1	0	0	3	0
Record player	2	12	0	3	0	2	3	17
Typewriter	0	8	0	2	0	0	13	17

The table suggests the following conclusions.

1. Pisaq ranks first in possession of modern artefacts, in 1969 as in 1964.

2. The rate of increase in possession of these objects has been much greater in Kuyo Chico than in Pisaq.

3. In 1964, according to these figures, only Pisaq and Kuyo Chico participated in the market economy of manufactured goods.

4. In 1969 Mask'a-Qotobamba and Chawaytirí had also entered into the market economy. The economic growth in Mask'a-Qotobamba is especially impressive.

In comparison with the totals for the seventeen villages, Pisaq is a little below average. Are the growth rates in Kuyo Chico, Mask'a-Qotobamba, and Chawaytirí faster than the average for communities in this larger study? Unfortunately, we cannot answer that question with our present data because of the low economic level of these communities in the baseline study. We can easily calculate (as 100 percent) the percentage of increase from 12 percent to 24 percent for sewing machines in Kuyo Chico, but the percentage increase from 0 percent to 8 percent in typewriters is incalculable. This conclusion holds with even greater force in Mask'a-Qotobamba and Chawaytirí, where, with only a single exception, the baseyear percentage is zero.

In spite of our inability to compare the rate of change of the communities of Cuzco with other villages, the figures presented in table 15 indicate that there has been a very impressive economic growth among the Indian population in the area we studied. This improvement has not been limited to Kuyo Chico.

Conclusions

The figures presented are many and complicated, but they tell a simple story.

We see that Kuyo Chico, after the termination of the program, had markedly lowered its level of confidence in the national government. We also noted a decrease of confidence in the municipality, controlled by Pisaq, although the level of confidence was very low even in 1964. The confidence in their community council continues very high, although we noted a slight decrease here also. As the program ended, the Kuyos' belief in their ability had not declined, nor had their trust in people.

In the items designed to measure modern-traditional attitudes, Kuyo Chico has maintained its position near the modern end of the continuum. In the area of civic or political activity and attitudes, on which we had many more items in 1969 than in 1964, Kuyo Chico occupies an outstanding position, not only in the Cuzco study but also in the seventeen village study. Although we see indications of a slight decline in internal solidarity, this still remains at a relatively high level. The respondents have a picture of their community as well organized and firmly oriented toward the future. They are optimistic about the future and have a great deal of confidence in their ability to overcome any problems which might arise for Kuyo Chico.

Indian-Mestizo relations appear to have improved in the five-year period, but one item is not sufficient to enable us to draw firm conclusions.

Has the program had a measurable impact outside of its principal base, Kuyo Chico? To answer this question, we

must distinguish between Chawaytirí and Mask'a-Qotobamba. The hacienda did not offer the same possibilities as
the Indian communities for the adoption of new ideas and
new forms of life. This structural difference may account for
the greater optimism and much higher index of civic activism
found in Mask'a-Qotobamba.

Can we say that the program in Kuyo Chico has caused this
apparent modernization in Mask'a-Qotobamba? To make such
a statement with adequate scientific evidence, we would need
measures of these communities taken before the time of intervention and perhaps also a comparative study of a control
group of similar communities in an area unaffected by the
program. At least we can say that the survey data tend to
support what we know from other evidence regarding the
impact of the program beyond Kuyo Chico (as, for example,
in the case of the termination of the Pisaq faenas).

However cautiously we may interpret the survey results,
we are left with one firm conclusion: the program has had an
impressive influence upon its immediate area of impact. In
the next chapter, we will analyze how this success was
achieved in a situation which posed a number of difficult
obstacles.

6

Lessons for Applied Anthropology

William F. Whyte and Oscar Núñez del Prado

In this final chapter we[1] will try to summarize the principles which have guided the program. We will also present what we have learned from the experience of Kuyo Chico. We hope in this way to be useful to others who hope to improve the human condition through applied anthropology. Our conclusions fall into twelve major points.

1. *Plan the work for the cultural context.*

The program was based on a thorough knowledge of the culture of the area. It was thus necessary to make an exhaustive study before launching action. This prerequisite necessarily delays the first intervention, but in the long run it is worth the time spent since it allows us to discover strategic points for intervention. Also it enables us to find the best ways to present the new elements we offer so as to encourage their serious consideration by the community.

2. *Think in terms of the geographic, economic, and social contexts.*

We realized that whatever significant change was introduced into Kuyo Chico would necessarily have an impact in

1. In this chapter, "we" refers to Núñez del Prado and his project staff.

the entire area. For example, since all the Indian communities in the area were exploited in the forced labor system of faenas, whatever action we took on this problem would necessarily have repercussions beyond Kuyo Chico. Furthermore, it was not our plan to limit our work to a single nucleus but rather to expand the impact, influencing the periphery through the natural process of diffusion from the action center. As they observed the actions carried out in Kuyo Chico, representatives of neighboring communities took the initiative in coming to ask the program for help, collaboration, and guidance in solving their problems, which seemed to them similar to those being resolved in Kuyo Chico.

The process of diffusion has also taken the form of imitation. Seeing Kuyo Chico raising money for the community through making tiles, other communities decided to enter into similar enterprises. Kuyo Grande constructed a kiln and roofed its school with its own tile production. Qotobamba also has its own kiln. Although the people of Amaru have not built a kiln, they have used the one in Kuyo Chico and have made enough tiles for a civic center built in their community. The home remodeling project in Kuyo Chico stimulated imitative efforts in Pisaq and elsewhere. And other Indian communities organized their community councils along the lines developed in Kuyo Chico.

3. *Combine the new with the traditional.*

Although in certain circumstances it may be necessary to get a community to abandon an old custom in order to introduce a new practice, generally it is more feasible to introduce the new in combination with the traditional. As the new elements are integrated with the traditional, the community more readily accepts elements which it associates with meanings which are valid in its own culture.

The introduction of modern medicine illustrates this principle. Generally such a change is seen as a struggle between doctor and native healer: a contest in which the doctor, with his powerful techniques and his scientific knowledge, tries to defeat the curandero and the superstitions which he represents. In this program, we conceived the relationship between the two specialists as one of collaboration. The doctor would first learn from the curandero, and then the curandero would learn from the doctor. The result has been the introduction of scientific medicine alongside certain traditional beliefs and practices. As they gain more experience with modern medicine, it is probable that the Indians will come to depend less on traditional medicine.

4. *The legal focus.*

Through examining customs and beliefs of a primitive tribe, the anthropologist can discover the native system of justice. In the study of a peasant community, the situation is different. Knowing that the laws of the country did not originate from within the community, the anthropologist sometimes tends to consider them as outside of his area of study. If he takes the laws into account, he tends to consider them as conservative forces, supporting the status quo.

The program recognized the difference between the laws themselves and the way they are applied in the field. The problem for the Indians was not a lack of good laws. In the Constitution and in various bodies of legislation there are provisions which accord with the highest humanitarian ideals. The problem was the lack of enforcement of such provisions or the way in which their enforcement was distorted.

The program recognized that, in certain circumstances, laws can serve as progressive and liberating forces, if the anthropologist knows how to get them enforced.

5. *The confrontation of power.*

Generally the applied anthropologist tries to be on good terms with everyone in his area of activity. Following this norm, even in tension-filled situations the anthropologist tries to initiate actions in an atmosphere of cordiality and persuasion. In the communities dominated by Pisaq, the Mestizo abuse of power had developed a system of exploitation of the Indian, who was not able to defend himself. Without a drastic change in the structure of power in the district, it would have been impossible to achieve much progress in Kuyo Chico. In a situation with basic differences of interests, a process of education regarding the relations that should prevail among human groups would have been useless. The only route then open to change was the confrontation between the power of the program and the local Mestizo power.

For this purpose, we used the coercive force of the law and also presented ourselves in the raiment of special powers. The fact that the program was sponsored by various governmental agencies in and of itself created the image of power. Our most direct lines of support were to the Peruvian Indian Institute in the Ministry of Labor and Indian Affairs and the University of Cuzco, but various government ministries had at least allowed their names to be used in sponsorship.

The circulars we sent to the authorities informed them of the nature and purposes of the program. With the stage thus set, we were in a position to pick our own battlefield. This we did with further circulars quoting the texts of laws protecting the rights of Indians and threatening with imprisonment and permanent disbarment from public office anyone who violated these laws.[2]

We planned to use the power which we had—or which people thought we had. The first test of power came in the Kuyo Chico assembly which was attended by the most prominent local Mestizo authorities. Our description of the laws and the reluctant Mestizo acknowledgment of the correctness of this information served to alarm the Mestizos and to encourage the Indians.

When we began the program, we were not at all sure that we would succeed in this power confrontation, but the fact that we took the offensive seems to have convinced people that we had more power than was in fact the case.

Our position also depended upon the outcome of a confrontation at a higher level, one with the prefect of the department of Cuzco, who had not been in sympathy with us. Presentation to the prefect of a copy of a document[3] implicating him in the illegal practice of recruitment of Indians for forced labor enabled us to get him to dismiss local officials hostile to us and to appoint men with whom we enjoyed good rela-

2. See Appendix.
3. See Appendix.

tions. Such changes helped to persuade both Mestizos and Indians that the program would be able to secure enforcement of the laws protecting Indians. The successful use of power and the symbols of power provided a necessary base upon which all of our projects depended, for without such confrontations the Indians would have had neither time, freedom, resources, nor spirit to improve their own conditions.

6. *Systems of community consultation.*

We sought the full participation of the adult population in the consideration of the problems of the community. This required not only the utilization of the existing channels of communication but also the creation of new channels of participation in the decision-making process. At first, to sound out community sentiment, we relied on our personal relationships with many individuals to carry out interviews and informal conversations. In the community assemblies which we started, there was a tendency to channel consultation through the personero (elected representative for dealing with government), but there were cases in which other community members took the initiative in putting forward ideas for discussion. In the community, there was no custom of open, community-wide discussion, and we had to stimulate the participation of the members by asking them questions. There was not only a reticence regarding active participation but also a reluctance to express open disagreement with someone. People tended to remain silent even when they disagreed. This tendency was even greater in cases where there was a difference in power and prestige; people especially hesitated to differ openly with opinions expressed by high-status members of the community. Through our efforts to stimulate participation, we noted a gradual increase in the number of speakers and also an increase in the frequency of expressing disagreements.

The women were especially backward in this regard. They followed the cultural norm that only the male has the right to state an opinion. To assure consideration of women's opinions, we had to let some time pass between the presentation of an idea in an assembly and the decision on that idea, so that the men could consult their spouses in the privacy of the home. While almost all the men attended the assemblies from the beginning, few women attended at first and those few never spoke. By 1967 we noted an increase in female attendance and some of the women had begun to speak, even occasionally expressing disagreement with the men.

7. *Patience: waiting for the people.*

The change agent naturally tends to judge the effectiveness of his own work on the basis of projects in process and projects completed. This tendency can make him impatient when a particular project does not progress at the desired rate. If he expresses this impatience, the community comes to look upon the project as the change agent's project rather than their own.

Our system was based upon informal discussions in which we nurtured certain ideas until the people took an interest in them and made them their own. In this way, they were more inclined to commit themselves to action. When, in the middle of a project, there was a marked loss of enthusiasm on the part of the people, we thought it best not to urge any action but rather to act as if the project were of no great interest to us. Then, after a time, when people began thinking about losing the potential benefits from the interrupted project, they were more likely to return to it.

Many of the projects have proceeded very slowly or have been abandoned for long periods of time. Such was the case with the irrigation ditch, which had seemed very important to the people. When they abandoned work on it, we showed no interest in its continuation. Then they began talking about the benefits they would lose if they did not finish the project, and they returned to work.

The same principle applied to our policy of not reaching decisions in a single community assembly. We felt that when the people took time to discuss the ideas informally in the home and with friends, the ideas themselves would take improved form, and the people would become more firmly committed to them.

8. *The selection of projects.*

147

The literature of community development advises the change agent to discover the desires of the community people and then help them to realize these goals. But how are community desires and needs to be determined?

In the Cuzco area, we had seen many cases where projects were selected in the following way. The community assembly would be presided over by individuals having some formal power, and it would be attended particularly by people of high prestige locally. There would also be a number of people who had been outside of the community for a long time and had brought back ideas from the towns and cities. These people would dominate the assembly and push ideas that were stylish in the outside world. The other members of the community might feel that the ideas did not meet their needs and desires, yet they refrained from expressing disagreement so as not to create problems between themselves and those of more status and influence. Thus what was known as "felt needs" was no more than the opinions of governors, lieutenant governors, mayors, and personeros who had some form of power and were thought of as the leaders of the community.

The program preferred to seek centers of social interest by means of interviews and informal discussions with a large number of people and, on this basis, make an analysis of the situation of the community as a whole. This process enabled us to find the interests and needs that had not been openly stated by the people yet that could serve as stepping stones to projects which could be developed to meet these and other community needs.

People may express a series of needs, some of which are impossible to satisfy. What they desire must be balanced against the possibilities of converting those desires into reality. The ideas of the change agent should not be imposed, but neither should the statements of community people be blindly accepted.

We felt that the first project should not necessarily be what the people wanted most but must be something which offered good possibilities of success. A failure on the first project could have had a disastrous effect on the commitment of the community to collaborate with the program. For this reason, we felt we could not escape the responsibility of assessing the feasibility of all projects on which we were to collaborate.

9. *The interrelations among projects.*

In applied anthropology, we should not think of projects in isolation. The failure of one project has the effect of discouraging the community. Success, on the other hand, stimulates the confidence of community members in themselves, strengthens their organization, and encourages them to think of new projects. The change agent should therefore be thinking how the immediate project may lead to new projects.

We have seen how home remodeling brought about the making of tiles and how that project influenced the inhabitants to undertake a series of more fundamental economic changes such as the construction of an irrigation ditch, reforestation, and so on. We have also seen how the economic and social changes depend on a change in the structure of power. Furthermore, without denying the importance of economic development, we have insisted that social and economic advancement must go together, since it is the social changes which make possible economic progress; economic advances, in turn, produce the rewards which stimulate social improvements.

10. *Organization by age categories.*

In the traditional Indian community, it is the old who have the power, and we had to adapt ourselves to that situation. In the literacy campaign, we did not start with the old people because we felt this would be too difficult, but neither did we start with the children, who could learn most easily. We started with married adults, as an intermediate age group with a position of some prestige in the community. We needed the understanding and support of this sector of the community, and we wanted to elevate their prestige by teaching them to read and write before their children. We also placed great emphasis on the adults between seventeen and twenty-five, more or less, in the sociability clubs.

The incorporation of this sector into active participation

in the program has resulted in a marked change in community leadership, according to age. The gerontocracy has been virtually eliminated, so that young adults now are elected to the community council. Thus, for example, the secretary is almost always a young man, although this is less common with the treasurer, who is expected to be a man with some economic resources.

11. *Recognition and formation of leadership.*

We were lucky in making our first contact in Kuyo Chico with a man of considerable prestige in the community. The position of Tomás Diaz surprised us. Since he had been chosen from outside, without consultation with the community, we had not expected him to have such influence in the community. When we recognized his actual prestige position, we sought to introduce our first interventions through him, while, in the meantime, we were creating new activities and new forms of organization which would produce new leaders. Tomás Diaz continues to be a person of great importance for the community, but other leaders have come forward to share the leadership with him. Thus the community depends less and less on the exceptional qualities of a single individual, which seems to us important for the future of a vigorous and well-organized community.

12. *The solidarity of the intervention team.*

If there is more than one change agent in the community, results will depend not simply on the sum of individual efforts but on the coordination of efforts in a spirit of teamwork. This objective is easier to achieve when the director has the right to choose his own collaborators. At first we had this opportunity, but later, when our budget proposals and other requests were not acted upon, we had to accept what was sent to us.

Our observations of the *Nucleos Escolares Campesinos* (peasant nuclear schools) showed us the importance of solidarity within the intervention team. A nuclear school was made up of personnel with different specialties: a supervisor of literacy, a supervisor of agricultural activities, a supervisor

of health, and various other members with specialized functions. Frequently the agricultural supervisor devotes himself
exclusively to some farm project, while the supervisor of
public health concentrates on that aspect, and the supervisor
of literacy simply concentrates on teaching his lessons. Not
only has there been no collaboration among the specialists,
but, even worse, each specialist competes against the others
to make his particular project stand out. One specialist may
even sabotage the work of others in order to gain personal
advantage. It is for this reason that the nuclear schools have
undergone a process of disintegration.

These observations led us to take seriously the task of
creating a spirit of cohesion within our intervention team. We
wanted the cohesion to have a sound emotional basis and to
link the members through affective ties as well as through
professional respect. Frictions inevitably arise among people
working together, so we had to be concerned that personal
grudges would not develop and undermine the team effort. A
disagreement, a correction of one member by another, or an
inopportune suggestion can precipitate frictions, but these
events lose their importance if the group develops a method
of dealing with them.

It was important to give members of the team the opportunity to seek and get explanations regarding what one member considered a personal affront by another. Such an explanation could satisfy the personal pride of the aggrieved
individual, and it might give him a deeper understanding of
the problem which had given rise to the offense. For this purpose, we held what we called "drainage sessions" once a
month.

Since the tensions could arise at different hierarchical
levels, during these sessions all of the members of the team
were considered of equal status. The director of the program
attended as an ordinary member, in order to receive the observations on his conduct in relation to the others. At first
there was great reticence and even careful selection of words
in phrasing criticisms of the director, but he proceeded to

encourage such expression, and little by little people came to speak frankly, without beating around the bush, no matter who was concerned.

With this system, the Kuyo Chico group was able to obtain a high sense of solidarity, which was not just reflected in personal relationships but also in the actions carried out by the team. Everyone became concerned with what was of interest to his companions, and helped them and collaborated with them, without sparing efforts and without expecting individual rewards.

Epilogue

On March 31, 1969, two officials of the Ministry of Labor and Communities delivered to the director of the program a note stating that it had been decided to close the Kuyo Chico project and requiring that all property of the project be turned over to the bearers of the note. This was done, and the most important resources, such as vehicles and machines, were turned over immediately to the Puno-Tambopata program. According to an oral agreement, Kuyo Chico was left with some tools and construction materials for the peasant hospital, so that the community would not be left without some of the resources indispensable for continuing at least some of the projects undertaken.

The Indians sent a petition to the president, requesting the formal transfer of these remaining assets to the community. Officials of the Ministry of Health in Cuzco have expressed interest in taking to Cuzco the medical and surgical equipment donated to Kuyo Chico by the canton of Geneva, on the grounds that their budget contains no item to cover the salary of a doctor for the Kuyo Chico hospital. Also, some functionaries of the Ministry of Education in Calca have come forward to try to persuade the Indians to cede the hospital site and building to the nuclear school of Pisaq. Both proposals have been vigorously rejected in community assemblies. The people say that they will build "their hospital" because they need a place where they can get medical care and from which they will not be turned away when they are sick. Later the Indians appealed repeatedly for help to General Enrique Valdez Angulo, president of the Corporation of Reconstruction and Development of Cuzco. His agreement has made possible the completion of two more wings of the peasant hospital. They also obtained from the corporation the services of engineers to make the necessary studies and plans for the provision of drinking water for the hospital and for the new village they hope to erect on adjoining lands, which they had reserved for that purpose.

What of the future? While our knowledge will not support any detailed predictions, we are encouraged to note that the spirit of the Indians of Kuyo Chico was not crushed by the abrupt closing of the government program. Our account of their reactions to this blow, together with the evidence of the 1969 survey, suggests that they remain dedicated to the defense of their rights as free citizens. With or without outside help, they will continue to carry on the struggle for greater access to the social and economic resources of modern Peru.

Appendix

Documents

1. Letter of September 19, 1959, regarding faenas, from Oscar Núñez del Prado to the governor of the district of Pisaq.

As you know, the National Plan for the Integration of the Aboriginal Population has established a program for the department of Cuzco, whose first pilot-project center is located in the communities of Amphay, Mask'a, Qotobamba, and Kuyo Chico, with an immediate area of influence in the communities of Viacha, Amaru, Sacaca, Paru-paru, Kuyo Grande, and others. Therefore, the personnel of this project have been working in the foregoing communities since the month of July of this year. The Ministry of Labor and Indian Affairs, through the Peruvian Indian Institute, has decided to select these communities as the initial area of operations of the aforementioned program, whose aims are to raise the moral, economic, and cultural level of the indigenous population, thus tending to incorporate it into the national life.

The magnitude of the labor to be carried out urgently requires that the Indians collaborate most closely with the project, dedicating the maximum possible of their time to the tasks contributing to their own betterment.

While carrying out a census and surveys in Mask'a and Qotobamba, we have been informed that your office has ordered obligatory faenas for the twenty-first and twenty-second of this month. We presume you meant the attendance of only persons who voluntarily wish to participate, since the decree of August 28, 1821, by General San Martín prohibits forced labor. This decree has been reiterated in circulars and laws such as no. 1183 which prohibits the authorities from contracting or pressing into service [*el enganche*] Indians for public works or private projects. On the other hand, our Constitution guarantees freedom of labor in article 55, as follows: "No one can be obliged to work without his free consent and without appropriate compensation."

We will appreciate it, Sr. Governor, if you will take the necessary measures so that your subordinate officers do not commit acts of violence, intimidation, or extraction of goods in order to force the Indians to participate against their will in the aforementioned faenas.

(Núñez del Prado sent a copy of this letter to the prefect of Cuzco, together with a letter describing more elaborately the aims of his program.)

2. Letter endorsing actions mentioned in document 1 above, signed by Manuel D. Velasco Núñez, Chief of the Executive Office of Programs for the Integration of the Aboriginal Population, September 26, 1959.

I have the pleasure of receiving your letter of the nineteenth . . . which you directed to the prefect of the department of Cuzco and to the governor of the district of Pisaq, in relation to the abuses victimizing the Indians within the zone of influence of the first pilot center of the Cuzco program.

I congratulate you for this patriotic and just initiative and wish you every success in your activities along this line. . . .

3. Circular sent October 5, 1959, by Oscar Núñez del Prado to the justice of the peace and other officials in Pisaq.

As I had the opportunity of informing you in Circular No. 1 of September 30, the applied anthropology program which I direct has assumed the exclusive responsibility for the application of programs of economic, social, and cultural development of the communities in the area of Pisaq. Therefore, and within my responsibility as representative of the Peruvian Indian Institute, which is charged with the protection of the freedom and of the rights of the Indians, in conformity with article 226 of the Penal Code, I direct myself to you to ask your most complete cooperation in order to carry out an energetic and dedicated labor, which will put an end once and for all to the abuses and outrages to which the Indians of this region have been victims.

It is not too much to indicate to you that existing legislation puts in our hands the necessary instruments for securing compliance with the law, as can be seen from the following provisions which I have the pleasure of transcribing for you.

Constitution of Peru, Art. 55. No one can be obliged to work without his free consent and without appropriate compensation.

Penal Code, Art. 225. He who, taking advantage of the ignorance and the moral weakness of certain classes of Indians and of other persons of like condition, subjects them to situations equivalent to or analogous to servitude, will be sent to the penitentiary or prison for not more than a year or will be fined in terms of his income from 30 to 90 days, and in any case will be barred from holding public office, according to article 27, for a period of not more than five years.

Law No. 605, Art. 1. Absolutely prohibited are the unremunerated and obligatory services which are known as "alcaldes de vara," "agentes," and "celadores municipales," "guardias de cárcel," "pongos," "semanaros," "mitanes," "alguaciles," "palmeros," "fiscales," etc. in the provinces of the southern region.

Art. 2. The civil, ecclesiastical, and military authorities who in any way, directly or indirectly, violate the provisions of the preceding article, will be immediately discharged and will be ineligible for the exercise of public functions for two years, without prejudice to criminal charges which can be made against them by citizens.

Law No. 1183, Art. 1. Political authorities of the Republic are prohibited from intervening in any way in the contracting of *peones* or workers of any classification for public works or private projects.

Art. 2. The aforementioned authorities who directly or through subordinates recruit or press into service [*enganchen*] Indians for public or private projects will suffer the penalty of imprisonment for one year.

Art. 3. Any citizen may bring charges concerning acts considered violations of the present law.

4. Statement testifying to violation of laws described above.

In Kuyo Chico, November 24, 1959, at 7:30 a.m., the following members of the community presented themselves: Andrés Becerra, Sergio Mamani, Felix Ttito, to charge that the municipal agent of Pisaq, Sr. Máximo Oblitas, was passing out money for pressing into service of *peones* for public works in Pisaq, advancing this money (for *enganche*) against the wishes of the Indian community members. Those making this charge presented themselves in order to return the money pressed upon them; for this reason and in view of the law, Sr. Oblitas has returned to collect the money given to these four persons. Sr. Oblitas states that he is only complying with the express orders of the governor, Don Luis Barrios and the mayor, Don Oscar Darío Montes.

(The statement is signed by the complainants and by Oscar Núñez del Prado and J. Hugo Contreras, the agricultural engineer attached to the project.)

5. Message sent by Governor Luis Barrios from his office authorizing the recruiting of workers for the hacienda of the prefect of Cuzco, in violation of Law No. 1183, quoted in statement 3 above. Note that this intercepted message enabled

Núñez del Prado to confront the prefect and secure the replacement of the governor and lieutenant governor.

The local official, Don Luis Suca of Kuyo Grande, will provide the facilities necessary to Don Lucio Cáceres so that he may contract people for work on the hacienda of the prefect of Cuzco, being accountable to this office.

Pisaq, April 6, 1960
Luis Barrios
(signature)

Index

Index

Impact of program—*Continued*
  in Pisaq ,107–8
  in Kuyo Chico, 108–18
Integration, concept of, 8–10
Indian-Mestizo relations, 6–11,
  16–23, 46–54, 113–15, 136–38
International Labor Organization,
  83
Irrigation project, 60
Indian Institute, Peruvian, xv, xvi,
  4–5, 8, 47

Justice:
  administration of, 14–15
  concepts of, 40–41

La Prensa, 3
Laws, 46, 51, 144
Linked projects, 58–65
Living conditions, 32–35
Local government. *See* Community
  government

Mangin, William, xv
Matos Mar, José, 119
Minka, 31–32
Mestizo-Indian relations. *See*
  Indian-Mestizo relations
Monge, Dr. Carlos, xv, xvi, 7
Mozo, 12, 20, 22, 108

National Plan for Integration of
  the Indian Population, 7–8, 48,
  72, 76, 84, 85, 106

Paternalism, 53, 114
Peace Corps, xvi, 60, 74, 106
Peasant movements, xviii–xix

Pongueaje, 3
Power, xiii, xvii–xix, xxiv, 13–15,
  46–54, 144
Prado, President Manuel, xxi
Prefect, 51
Priest. *See* Church

Q'ero, 3–5
Quechua, xv, 12, 13, 56, 69, 120
Quevedo, Sergio, 5, 7

Religion, 87–89
Ritual kinship. See *Compadrazgo*
Román, Pelegrín, 8, 85

Sánchez, Rodolfo, 5, 7, 70, 75
SECPANE, 45
SCIPA, 60
SCIPS, 78
Spiritual world, 35–43

Teachers, 51–52, 71–72
Teamwork (of project staff), 95–
  101
Tile project, 59–62
Traditionalism, 128–29
Tuberculosis, 56, 78

Usurpation of land, 108

Vázquez, Mario, xv, xviii, 4
Velasco Nuñez, Manuel, 4, 7
Vicos, xvii–xx
Voting, 76–77

Williams, Lawrence K., 119
Work, orientation to, 125–26
World Health Organization, 83

162